C000154830

ESSENTIAL
TUNISIA

★ Best places to see 34–55

■ Featured sight

Tunis and the North 79–110

Central Tunisia 131–158

Cap Bon 111–130

Jerba and the South 159–186

Original text by Peter Lilley
Updated by Sylvie Franquet

© AA Media Limited 2009   Series Editor Karen Kemp
First published 2007   Series Designer Sharon Rudd
Revised 2009   Cartographic Editor Anna Thompson

ISBN: 978-0-7495-6132-1

Published by AA Publishing, a trading name of AA Media Limited, whose registered office is Fanum House, Basing View, Basingstoke, Hampshire RG21 4EA. Registered number 06112600.

Colour separation: MRM Graphics Ltd
Printed and bound in Italy by Printer Trento S.r.l.

A03804
Maps in this title produced from mapping © MAIRDUMONT / Falk Verlag 2009

About this book

Symbols are used to denote the following categories:

- ✚ map reference to maps on cover
- ✉ address or location
- ☎ telephone number
- 🕐 opening times
- 👋 admission charge
- 🍴 restaurant or café on premises or nearby
- Ⓜ nearest underground train station
- 🚌 nearest bus/tram route
- 🚉 nearest overground train station
- ⛴ nearest ferry stop
- ✈ nearest airport
- ❓ other practical information
- ℹ tourist information
- ➤ indicates the page where you will find a fuller description

This book is divided into five sections.

The essence of Tunisia pages 6–19
Introduction; Features; Food and drink; Short break including the 10 Essentials

Planning pages 20–33
Before you go; Getting there; Getting around; Being there

Best places to see pages 34–55
The unmissable highlights of any visit to Tunisia

Best things to do pages 56–75
Places to picnic; places to take the children; top activities; best souqs and markets; best archaeological sites and more

Exploring pages 76–186
The best places to visit in Tunisia, organized by area

Maps
All map references are to the maps on the covers. For example, Hammamet has the reference ✚ E4 – indicating the grid square in which it is to be found.

Admission prices
Inexpensive (under 3D)
Moderate (3D–6D)
Expensive (over 6D)

Hotel prices
Price are per room per night:
£ budget (under 30D);
££ moderate (30D–80D);
£££ expensive to luxury (over 80D)

Restaurant prices
Price for a three-course meal per person without drinks:
£ budget (under 10D);
££ moderate (10D–25D);
£££ expensive (over 25D)

Contents

THE ESSENCE OF...

6 – 19

PLANNING

20 – 33

BEST PLACES TO SEE

34 – 55

BEST THINGS TO DO

56 – 75

EXPLORING...

76 – 186

The essence of...

Introduction   8–9

Features   10–11

Food and drink   12–15

Short break   16–19

Many visitors have been drawn to Tunisia for its sunny climate and its bargain beach-resort holidays: the white sandy beaches are glorious, the sea a clear turquoise, and some of the resorts are among the best the Mediterranean has to offer. But in many ways this is perhaps the least this relatively small country has to offer. Those who venture away from the coast will discover a wealth of archaeological monuments, gorgeous white-washed médinas, a vast expanse of desert and lush oases in the south and green oak forests in the north. The Tunisians are some of the friendliest people in North Africa, and the exciting spicy cuisine, based on fresh local produce and a lot of fresh fish and seafood, comes as a delightful surprise.

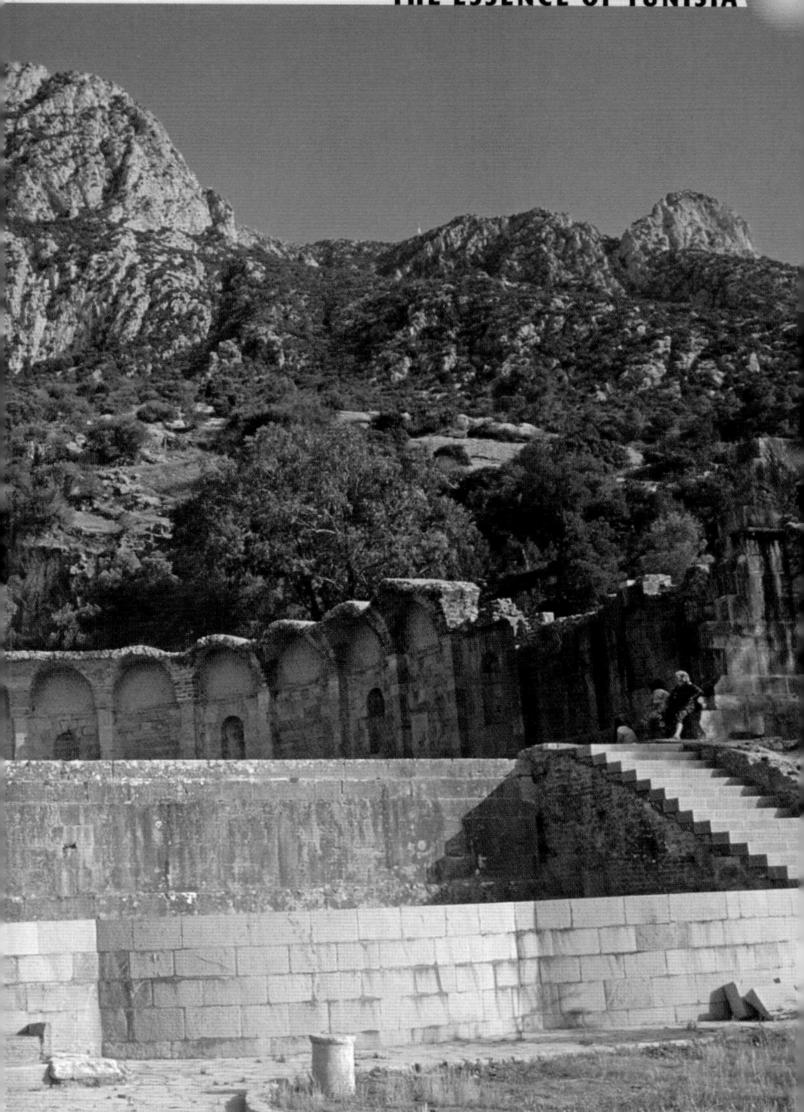

features

Tunisia is a mainstream Mediterranean holiday destination, but it still attracts a lot of first-time visitors. If there's a choice, go in late spring or summer to one of the major centres such as Tunis, Sousse or Sfax. Drop the bags and venture straight out into the streets. Late afternoon is the most magical time of day: birds chatter in the trees on the main boulevards, the whole town seemingly comes out for a stroll and a snack or an ice cream, and in the smoky bars and cafés the men chat over a coffee, cards and a *chicha,* with perhaps a bottle of Celtia, Tunisia's most popular beer.

In the mysterious médinas, there is the feeling that a thousand secrets lurk behind every studded door; shops and stalls in the souqs and surrounding streets spring to life to serve the homeward bound with the freshest food. Fish are only minutes out of the sea, bread is baked on the spot and stacks of colourful vegetables are haggled over with shouts and handshakes.

It is easy to get away from it all in Tunisia, since there are very few major cities, and much of the rest of the country is sparsely populated. The country has only a handful of national parks and municipal gardens, but there are few restrictions on wandering in the countryside.

GEOGRAPHY
● Tunisia is the northernmost country in Africa; it lies just 80km (50 miles) southwest of Sicily. It measures 750km (465 miles) from north to south but only 150km (93 miles) from west to east, making it slightly larger than the US state of Florida.
● The northern and eastern coastlines are bordered by the Mediterranean, while much of the southern half of the country is within the Sahara Desert.

CLIMATE
● Summers are hot and dry. In July and August daytime temperatures on the east coast average 30°C (86°F) with 12 hours of sunshine. In the desert it can reach 45°C (113°F).
● In the north, winters are mild but quite wet, with occasional snow.
● Daytime temperatures in the south average 20°C (68°F), but fall rapidly at night to near freezing.

PEOPLE
● Tunisia has a population of about 10.3 million.
● More than half the people are under 18 and more than 35 per cent under 14, one of the youngest populations in the world.
● About 99 per cent of the population is Sunni Muslim, with tiny Christian and Jewish minorities.
● More than 60 per cent of the population is urban.

LANGUAGE
● Arabic is the official language, but almost everyone speaks some French.
● It is rare to find English or German spoken outside the main beach resorts.
● A few centres of indigenous Berber culture survive in southern Tunisia, where the people still speak the Berber language.

food & drink

Tunisian cuisine is typically North African and is influenced by Arab traditions as well as by its Berber culture, using powerful spices and plenty of vegetables and fish. The French colonial heritage has produced some excellent wines.

Although international food is served in most Tunisian tourist hotels, many holidaymakers will want to try some of the local cuisine. The Arabs and French have all had an influence on the country's cooking. With so much coast, fish is given pride of place on any menu, and restaurant owners compete with each other to display the freshest catch. Bream, grouper, sea bass and red mullet are among the most widely available, while seafood speciality dishes are based on prawns, lobster and squid. Tuna is added to everything – even when you ask for a vegetarian pizza or green salad. Eggs are another staple ingredient which appear unexpectedly in many dishes.

A TYPICAL TUNISIAN MEAL
In all but the cheapest restaurants customers are nearly always welcomed with complimentary hors d'oeuvres which may be as simple as a bowl of black olives and some delicious crusty bread.

In most places the bread will also be accompanied with a small saucer of fiery red *harissa* paste made from hot chillies (caution is advised).

A popular starter is the famous *brik*, a unique Tunisian dish, which consists of a thin, crispy pancake filled with a runny egg and often topped with fresh herbs, prawns, potato or tuna. It can only really be eaten with the fingers, but beware of the yolk making a sudden and undignified escape. Safer starters include *ojja*, made from scrambled eggs mixed with tomatoes, pimentos, peppers and garlic. *Mechouia* is a salad of grilled peppers, chillies and tomatoes, mixed with olive oil and served with hard-boiled eggs and tuna. *Chorba* is a spicy soup of tomatoes, onions and *harissa* with wheat.

The obvious main course is couscous, a tasty vegetable, meat or fish stew served on a bed of steamed semolina grains, Tunisia's national dish. *Mesfuf* is a sweet couscous made with nuts and raisins. *Mechoui* (not to be confused with *mechouia*) is traditionally a whole roast lamb, but it can refer to a shoulder or leg of lamb. *Merguez* are spicy lamb sausages.

Dessert is often a choice of fresh fruit or sweet pastries such as *baklava* (filo pastry with nuts and honey) or *kab el ghazal* (a horn-shaped pastry filled with almonds).

WHAT TO DRINK

Although Tunisia is a Muslim country, alcohol is quite freely available in hotels and restaurants in Tunis and the main beach resorts. Bars outside hotels are frequented mainly by men, which may make women feel uncomfortable. Two micro-breweries in Hammamet and Port El Kantaoui make their own German-style beer, but most bars serve the Tunisian beer Celtia, or the new Heineken brewed in Cap Bon.

Tunisian wines are generally pleasant to drink, with the best wines coming from the Cap Bon region. There are several new winemakers and the quality is improving. Old favourites like the red Magon, the full-bodied Vieux Magon and the very dry Blanc de Blanc are still good.

Tunisia's best-known spirits are *thibarine*, a sweet, aromatic date liqueur and *boukha*, a clear fig brandy.

short break

If you have only a short time to visit Tunisia and would like to take home some unforgettable memories, you can do something local and capture the real flavour of the country. The following suggestions will give you a wide range of sights and experiences that won't take very long, won't cost very much and will make your visit very special.

● **Head inland** to see the real Tunisia, with its magnificent countryside and spectacular Roman ruins.

● **Walk off the main drag** of the Tunis médina (➤ 83) and get lost in its fascinating alleys long enough to discover an elegant minaret or a beautiful medersa (theological school).

● **Buy a piece of pottery** such as a vase, large plate or bowl. Blue and white are the traditional colours, while fish decorations add extra value.

Nabeul (▶ 118–121) and Guellala (▶ 162–163) are the major centres, but pottery is on sale almost everywhere.

● **Go spicy** and eat a fried chilli or the fiery *harissa* sauce with just about everything.

● **Go to sleep** with a sweet-smelling sprig of jasmine on your pillow. The women wear garlands of the flower around their necks, while the men sometimes tuck a neat little bunch behind their ear.

● **Follow a couscous** with a strong syrupy mint tea with pine nuts, served with *baklava* – layers of filo pastry with crushed almonds or pistachios.

● **Ride a camel** at sunset in Douz (➤ 169), the gateway to the Sahara Desert.

● **Sleep in an underground cave** in the bizarre landscape of Matmata (➤ 172), the set of a *Star Wars* movie.

● **Listen to the *muezzin*** calling the Muslim faithful to prayer five times a day. Many mosques are closed to non-Muslims, but outside prayer hours you may be able to approach as far as the door for a glimpse.

● **Take home** a bunch of fresh Tunisian dates, some of the best in the world.

Planning

Before you go   22–25

Getting there   26–27

Getting around   28–29

Being there   30–33

Before you go

WHEN TO GO

JAN	FEB	MAR	APR	MAY	JUN	JUL	AUG	SEP	OCT	NOV	DEC
16°C	17°C	20°C	21°C	23°C	27°C	30°C	32°C	29°C	25°C	22°C	17°C
61°F	63°F	68°F	70°F	73°F	81°F	86°F	90°F	84°F	77°F	72°F	63°F

High season   Low season

Northern Tunisia has a typical Mediterranean climate with hot, dry summers and cool, wet winters. In January, the Kroumirie and Teboursouk mountain ranges to the west may get a little snow. It gets progessively hotter and drier the further south you go.

Annual rainfall ranges from 1,000mm (40 inches) in the north to 180mm (7 inches) in the south, while the Grand Erg Occidental in the interior may have no rain for years at a time.

The best time to visit coastal regions is between early May and late September. The interior is best visited during the spring or autumn.

See page 11 for more information on the climate.

WHAT YOU NEED

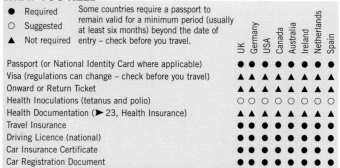

● Required
○ Suggested
▲ Not required

Some countries require a passport to remain valid for a minimum period (usually at least six months) beyond the date of entry – check before you travel.

	UK	Germany	USA	Canada	Australia	Ireland	Netherlands	Spain
Passport (or National Identity Card where applicable)	●	●	●	●	●	●	●	●
Visa (regulations can change – check before you travel)	▲	▲	▲	▲	▲	▲	▲	▲
Onward or Return Ticket	▲	▲	▲	▲	▲	▲	▲	▲
Health Inoculations (tetanus and polio)	○	○	○	○	○	○	○	○
Health Documentation (► 23, Health Insurance)	▲	▲	▲	▲	▲	▲	▲	▲
Travel Insurance	●	●	●	●	●	●	●	●
Driving Licence (national)	●	●	●	●	●	●	●	●
Car Insurance Certificate	●	●	●	●	●	●	●	●
Car Registration Document	●	●	●	●	●	●	●	●

WEBSITES

www.tourismtunisia.com
www.tunisiaonline.com
www.tunisair.com.tn/

www.tunisia.com
www.cometotunisia.co.uk
www.lexicorient.com/tunisia

TOURIST OFFICES AT HOME

UK Tunisian National Tourist Office ✉ 77A Wigmore Street, London W1H 9LJ ☎ (020) 7224 5598

USA Tunisian National Tourist Board ✉ 1515 Massachusetts Avenue NW, Washington, DC 20005 ☎ (202) 466 2546

Canada Tunisian Tourist Office ✉ 1253 McGill College, Suite 655, Montreal, Quebec H3B 2Y5 ☎ (514) 397 1182

Spain Oficina Nacional del Turismo Tunesino ✉ Plaza de Espana 18, Torre de Madrid 28008, Planta 4, Oficina 1, Madrid ☎ (341) 548-1435

France Office National du Tourisme Tunisien ✉ 32 avenue de l'Opera, Paris 75002 ☎ (331) 4742-7267

HEALTH INSURANCE

Don't be tempted to skimp on travel insurance. If you fall ill, all major tourist hotels or a pharmacist should be able to recommend a good doctor, although any treatment would have to be paid for and then reclaimed. Keep all your receipts. Most tourist hotels should be able to recommend a reputable dentist. Any treatment you have will need to be paid for, then reclaimed on your insurance at a later date – if possible pay by credit card. Have a thorough dental check-up before leaving home.

TIME DIFFERENCES

GMT	Tunisia	Spain	USA (NY)	USA (West Coast)	Sydney
12 noon	1PM	1PM	7AM	4AM	10PM

Tunisian local time is one hour ahead of Greenwich Mean Time (GMT+1) all year round, which means that flying from Britain in summer there is no time difference, while in winter clocks have to be put forward one hour.

NATIONAL HOLIDAYS

1 Jan *New Year's Day*	9 Apr *Martyrs' Day*	25 Jul *Republic Day*
18 Jan *Revolution Day*	1 May *International*	13 Aug *Women's Day*
20 Mar *Independence Day*	*Labour Day*	7 Nov *Commemoration*
21 Mar *Youth Day*	1 Jun *National Day*	*Day*

WHAT'S ON WHEN

As a Muslim country, Tunisia celebrates a number of national festivals related to Islam. The dates of these religious events are calculated according to the Muslim calendar, which is lunar, making dates 11 days earlier each year. By far the most important festival is the holy month of Ramadan, adhered to by most Tunisians. During Ramadan, Muslims abstain from eating, drinking and smoking from sunrise to sunset. Every evening there is a feast, with eating and drinking late into the night. At the end of Ramadan is one of the biggest holidays in Tunisia: a three-day feast known as *Aid al-Seghir*. Some tourists avoid travelling during this period.

Forty days after that is another major celebration, the *Aid al-Kebir*, or *Aid al-Adha*, commemorating Abraham's devotion to God, who told him to sacrifice his son. God 'stayed' his hand when He saw that Abraham was prepared to carry out the order. Most people return to their home town or village for a family feast, and everything is closed for at least two days.

Mouled is a celebration of the Prophet Muhammad's birthday, and *Al-Hijra* is the Muslim New Year.

The following are among the most popular local festivals.

February *Olive Festival:* Kalaa Kebira (near Sousse).

March–April *Ksour Festival:* Berber traditions and folklore; Tataouine.

Orange Blossom Festival: a programme of cultural events; Nabeul and Menzel Bouzelta.

May *Matanza:* incredible tuna harvest, where tuna are caught en masse on their annual migration to spawn along the coast; Sidi Daouad in Cap Bon.

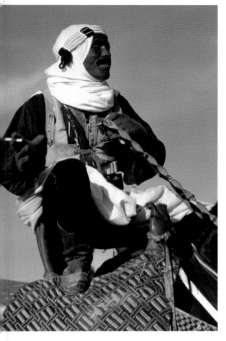

June *Falconry Festival:* falcons trained by villagers take part in a series of competitions to catch partridge and quail before being released into the wild; El Haouaria.

Ulysses Festival: folklore festival including a re-enactment of the arrival in Jerba of Ulysses; island of Jerba.

July–August *Classical Music Festival:* El Jem.

Music Festival: week-long festival of *maalouf* music, which was exported to North Africa by Andalucian refugees between the 12th and the 15th centuries; Testour (75km/46 miles southwest of Tunis).

Festival of Carthage: the biggest cultural festival in Tunisia. Dance, film, theatre and musical events, staged within the restored Roman theatre; Carthage.

Dougga Festival: theatrical performances in the spectacular setting of the Roman theatre within the archaeological site; Dougga.

Festival of Theatre: folk music, dancing and plays; Sousse.

International Jazz Festival: Tabarka.

Jerba Folklore Festival: held every other year (even years); Jerba.

International Festival: music, dance and theatre; Monastir.

September *Cavalry Festival:* displays of horsemanship; Kairouan.

November *Date Harvest Festival:* Kebili.

Festival of Tozeur: oasis folklore and traditions; Tozeur.

International Film Festival: held biennially (even years); Carthage.

December *International Festival of the Sahara:* attracts up to 50,000 Bedouin, nomads and tourists for camel races and folklore displays. Held in the desert on the edge of town; Douz.

Getting there

BY AIR

Tunis-Carthage International Airport

20–25 minutes

12 minutes

8km (5 miles) from city centre

Monastir-Skanès International Airport

20 minutes

10 minutes

15 minutes

10km (6 miles) from city centre

Tunisia has six international airports: Tunis-Carthage, Monastir-Skanès, Jerba-Zarzis, Tozeur, Tabarka and Sfax-Thyna. There are no direct flights from North America, but regular flights from London and Paris.

Tunis-Carthage International Airport is 8km (5 miles) from Tunis city centre. You can get there by yellow taxi, private taxi or bus.

Monastir-Skanès Airport is 10km (6 miles) west of Monastir. You can get to Monastir using one of the yellow taxis or there is a metro station outside the airport offering a service from Sousse and Mahdia via Monastir and Skanès Airport.

BY SEA

There are ferry services to Tunis from Marseille in France (www.ctn.com.tn) and from Genoa, La Spezia, Naples and Trapani in Italy (www3.gvn.it). This travel option is particularly popular with European visitors who wish to bring their car with them. You should make reservations well in advance.

DRIVING
- Drive on the right.
- Speed limit on motorways: 110kph (68 miles)
- Speed limit on main roads: 90kph (56 miles)
- Speed limit in built-up areas: 50kph (31 miles)
- Seat belts are compulsory for the driver and front-seat passengers on roads between cities.
- Random breath-testing does not take place, but there are a lot of traffic police and local people are regularly asked to produce their papers. You may be asked for your passport, but it is almost unheard of for tourists to be booked unless they cause an accident.
- Fuel is sold as super, regular and *essence sans plomb* (lead-free petrol). Although petrol stations are plentiful, never make the mistake of running short on fuel, especially when driving in more remote areas.
- Do not expect to be able to call a motoring assistance organization if you break down – although some of the major international car rental companies will provide replacement vehicles and help. Garage mechanics can normally fix most problems. Punctured tyres are common, so if planning a long journey take food and blankets.

Getting around

PUBLIC TRANSPORT

Internal flights There is not much demand for domestic air travel in Tunisia. The two busiest routes are between Tunis and Tozeur, and Tunis and Jerba, which is used as a major gateway into Libya. All internal flights are operated by TunInter.

Trains Tunisia's small but very efficient rail network is operated by the Societé Nationale des Chemins de Fer Tunisiens (SNCFT; www.sncft.com.tn). The main line runs north to south from Tunis to Gabès. The whole route is serviced by three trains daily; Tunis to Sousse, eight trains daily; Tunis to Sfax, six trains daily. Other lines run from Tunis to Bizerte, and Tunis to Béja and Jendouba. Trains offer three classes: second, first and comfort. Some have air-conditioned carriages. Train fares are relatively inexpensive. A *Carte Bleue* offers unlimited rail travel for one, two or three weeks.

Buses The Société Nationale de Transport Interurbain (SNTRI; www.sntri.com.tn) has a wide network of bus routes. Bigger towns usually have a central bus station. Local buses are usually filled to the brim, especially on market days when you may find yourself sharing the journey with chickens or sheep.

Urban transport Tunis has a *métro leger* (tram) network and a very limited suburban rail service connecting the capital with Carthage and La Marsa. Services are punctual if not exactly frequent. There is also a metro service between Sousse and Mahdia which

is useful for visitors staying at hotels in Skanès.

TAXIS

Taxis are plentiful in most cities and relatively good value. All have meters and charge 50 per cent more between 9pm and 6am. Always insist that the meter is switched on when you get in, as some drivers will try to charge tourists a higher fare.

Louages (shared taxis) leave when the vehicle is full. The fare is split between all the passengers.

CAR RENTAL

Car rental in Tunisia is expensive. Even vehicles from international rental companies can be poorly maintained, and there are many potential hazards, from people driving at night without lights to pedestrians walking out into the road without looking.

FARES AND TICKETS

Domestic airline tickets can be bought online (www.tuninter.com.tn, in French), from travel agents or at the airport. Train tickets can be bought online (www.sncft.com.tn, in French) and at railway stations, and come in three categories: 2nd class, 1st class (more spacious and upholstered reclining seats) and *confort* (the same but fewer people). Intercity buses are best booked in advance, particularly during public holidays, from the bus station or some travel agents.

There are few travel concessions for foreign visitors.

Museums and archaeological sites normally, but not always, offer some reductions to students with valid identification. Senior citizens pay the normal adult entry price.

Being there

TOURIST OFFICES

Bizerte ✉ 1 rue de Constantinople, Old Port ☎ 72 432897
Hammamet ✉ Avenue Habib Bourguiba ☎ 72 280423
Jerba ✉ Boulevard de l'Environnement ☎ 75 650016
Kairouan ✉ Place du Bassin des Aghlabites ☎ 77 231897

Monastir ✉ Zone Touristique de Skanès ☎ 73 520205
Sousse ✉ 1 avenue Habib Bourguiba ☎ 73 225157
Tabarka ✉ 32 avenue Habib Bourguiba ☎ 78 671491
Tozeur ✉ 89 avenue Abdul Kacem Chabbi ☎ 76 454503
Tunis ✉ 1 avenue Mohamed V ☎ 71 341077

MONEY

The monetary unit of Tunisia is the dinar, which is divided into 1,000 millimes. There is a one dinar coin and coins for 5, 10, 20, 50, 100 and 500 millimes. Banknotes come in 5D, 10D and 20D denominations. It is illegal to import or export dinars, so you will be unable to obtain local currency in advance.

You can exchange cash and travellers' cheques at most banks and major hotels. The best currencies to use are pounds sterling, euros (€) or US dollars. Major cities have many ATMs. Credit cards are widely accepted throughout Tunisia, especially at tourist destinations.

POSTAL AND INTERNET SERVICES

Post offices are known as PTTs (Poste. Telephone. Telegraphe) and are well-represented throughout the country. They sell stamps, although

TIPS/GRATUITIES

Yes ✓   No ✗

Restaurants	✓	10%
Cafés/bars	✓	a few coins
Taxis	✓	optional
Tour guides	✓	
Porters	✓	up to 3D
Chambermaids	✓	up to 3D
Toilets	✓	optional

these can also be bought from hotels, newsagents and kiosks. Postboxes are generally small and yellow. Postcards and letters to Europe can take about a week to arrive, but the service is very reliable.

Public access to the internet in Tunisia is handled by the government-owned Publinet, with internet cafés in most sizeable towns. If you have your own portable computer, only the upmarket hotels have internet access in the rooms.

TELEPHONES

Public phones can be found at the post office, or in one of the many Taxiphone or Publitel offices. There will be several booths under one roof with an attendant to give change. You can make a direct dial international call very easily using one dinar coins or a phonecard. Some shops have public phones, usually indicated by a blue sign.

Emergency telephone numbers
Police 197   **Ambulance** 190
Fire 198

International dialling codes
From Tunisia to: **USA** and **Canada** 00 1
UK 00 44   **Australia** 00 61
Germany 00 49   **Netherlands** 00 31

EMBASSIES AND CONSULATES
UK ☎ 71 108700   **Germany** ☎ 71 786455
USA ☎ 71 107000   **France** ☎ 71 105000

ELECTRICITY
The voltage is generally 220/240 volts, with 110 volts in some remote areas. Sockets take two-round-pin plugs so an international adaptor is needed for most non-continental European appliances. A transformer is needed for appliances using 100–120 volts.

HEALTH AND SAFETY
Sun advice The sun can be very hot, particularly between June and September in the main beach resorts and the deep south. Wear a hat,

loose cotton clothing and high-factor sunscreen. Drink plenty of bottled water, avoid excess alcohol and caffeine and restrict the amount of time spent in direct sunlight.

Drugs Pharmacists are very knowledgeable. Their shops are generally well supplied, although it is always worth checking the date stamp on medicines, which can deteriorate quickly in the heat. Pharmacists can supply drugs for many minor complaints such as sore throat, upset stomach or diarrhoea.

Personal safety Tunisia is a very safe country with a relatively low crime rate. Sadly, petty thieving is on the increase, particularly in busy resorts. Beware of groups of small children distracting you with posies of flowers or cheap souvenirs.

- Beware of pickpockets, especially in crowded markets and souqs.
- Keep cameras and other valuables in closed bags.
- Do not carry more money and valuables than you need.
- Make use of hotel safes.
- Do not walk alone around médinas at night.
- Women should dress modestly, covering themselves when away from the beach or hotel.

OPENING HOURS

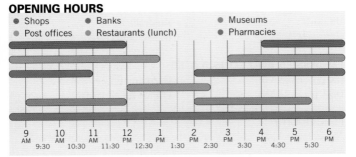

- Shops
- Post offices
- Banks
- Restaurants (lunch)
- Museums
- Pharmacies

9 AM | 9:30 | 10 AM | 10:30 | 11 AM | 11:30 | 12 PM | 12:30 | 1 PM | 1:30 | 2 PM | 2:30 | 3 PM | 3:30 | 4 PM | 4:30 | 5 PM | 5:30 | 6 PM

In the summer, shops may stay closed for much of the afternoon, then reopen in the evening when it is cooler. During Ramadan, working hours are also generally shortened. Many museums and archaeological sites are closed on Mondays. Pharmacies are found in every village and are well-stocked, with staff speaking fluent French. In large towns, there will be a pharmacy open 24 hours a day, but closed on Sundays.

LANGUAGE

Tunisia is almost bilingual. Although the official language is Arabic, nearly everyone speaks some French and it is increasingly common among wealthier classes and the business community for people to speak 'Frarabic'– a rather odd mixture of the two. Not content with two languages under their belt, a lot of young Tunisians are also learning English or German. Tourists can do their bit by learning a few words of Arabic, which is well worth the effort as it usually brings instant friendship.

yes/no	*oui/non*	*naam/la'a*
please/thank you	*s'il vous plaît/merci*	*birabee/shukran*
hello/goodbye	*bonjour/au revoir*	*assalama/bislémah*
good morning	*bonjour*	*sabah el khir*
good evening	*bon soir*	*missa el khir*
excuse me	*pardon*	*samahanee*
how are you?	*ça va?*	*ashnooa ahwalik?*
open/closed	*ouvert/ferme*	*mahoul/msaker*
bank	*une banque*	*bank*
post office	*une poste*	*bousta* or *barid*
hotel	*un hôtel*	*otel/fondouk*
I want a room	*Je voudrais une chambre*	*B'gheet oda/beet*
Can I look at it?	*Est-ce qu'on peut la voir*	*Yoomkin ashoofa?*
How much?	*Combien?*	*Kaddésh?*
shower	*la douche*	*doosha*
the bill	*l'addition*	*el-hisaab*
fish/meat	*poisson/viande*	*samak* or *huut/lahm*
vegetables/fruit	*légumes/fruit*	*khodra/fawakih*
water/wine	*de l'eau/vin*	*maa/sharab*
tea/coffee	*thé/café*	*shay/kahwa*
bread	*pain*	*khoubz*
airport	*l'aéroport*	*al-matar*
bus/car	*l'autobus/la voiture*	*autobees/sayara*
train station	*gare*	*mahata el tran*
garage/petrol	*le garage/l'essence*	*garage/benzeen*

Best places to see

Dougga   36–37

El Jem   38–39

Îles Kerkennah   40–41

Jebel Ichkeul National Park
(Parc National de l'Ichkeul)   42–43

Kairouan   44–45

Ksar Ouled Soltane   46–47

Musée du Bardo, Tunis   48–49

Nefta   50–51

Sidi Bou Saïd   52–53

Thermes d'Antonin   54–55

1 Dougga

Tunisia's best-preserved and most spectacular Roman ruins have a dramatic setting on a hillside with wide views of the surrounding countryside.

The Roman town of Dougga, a UNESCO World Heritage Site, was built on the site of the ancient settlement of Thugga, which had become the seat of the Numidian king Massinissa in the 2nd century BC. Dougga prospered under Roman rule and at its peak is thought to have had a population of 10,000 people. In the early 1950s residents were moved to the nearby purpose-built village of Nouvelle Dougga.

Fervent archaeologists will find Dougga worth a full day's visit, and even those with a limited interest need to allow at least two hours just to see the main buildings. It is advisable – particularly in summer – to arrive as early as possible to avoid the crowds and intense midday heat.

The heavily restored Roman theatre, cut into the hillside, is the most complete of any in Tunisia and is used for the Dougga Festival in summer. There is a magnificent view over the surrounding wheat fields and olive groves from the impressive Temple of Saturn, dedicated to the sun god Baal Hammon. The centrepiece of the nearby Plaza of the Winds is a compass-like wind-indicator inscribed with the names of the 12 Roman winds. Dougga's star attraction is the well-preserved Capitol, built in AD166 and dedicated to Jupiter, Juno and Minerva. Near the Arch of Severus is the attractive Temple of Caelestis, with a beautiful semicircular portico. The House of Trifolium is thought to have been the town's brothel; the latrines immediately beside it have been very well preserved.

✚ L7 ✉ 110km (68 miles) southwest of Tunis 🕐 Daily 8–7 (8:30–5:30 in winter) 🖐 Inexpensive 🍴 Small café (£) near main entrance. Restaurant Mercure (£–££) near ticket office at Nouvelle Dougga (closed Mon in winter) 🚌 Hourly daytime services from Tunis to El Kef which stop at Nouvelle Dougga 3km (2 miles) from site. Difficult to reach site without a car. Taxis from Teboursouk ❓ Dougga International Festival – theatre and concerts in the amphitheatre (Jul–Aug); www.tourismtunisia.com

2 El Jem

The amphitheatre at El Jem is one of the Roman Empire's greatest legacies to Tunisia.

El Jem is only slightly smaller than the Colosseum in Rome, but it is better preserved and more imposing, though situated incongruously at the end of a street of modern houses. If it were near a major European holiday destination there is little doubt it would be packed solid with visitors year-round, so try to see it soon before the crowds get there. Early morning is a good time to take photographs and dusk is particularly atmospheric.

Pleasingly, there are very few signs or notices inside the amphitheatre, making it easier to imagine the colourful festivals or the bloody dawn-to-dusk gladiatorial contests that were held here. The gladiators – often simply petty thieves, debtors or prisoners – would be pitted against each other or against wild animals to fight to the death.

Built between AD230 and 238 in the busy market town of Thysdrus, the amphitheatre could seat crowds of more than 30,000. Measuring 149m (489ft) long by 124m (407ft) wide, even today it would be considered an impressive building achievement, but having been constructed without modern equipment, it is an awesome feat of engineering. In the absence of suitable materials locally, blocks of sandstone were transported from quarries 30km (19 miles) away, while water was carried 15km (9 miles) in an underground aqueduct.

El Jem **archaeological museum** has attractive 3rd-century mosaics. Behind the museum is Maison d'Africa, a complete and stunning Roman villa with garden and pool.

✚ R20 ✉ 70km (43 miles) south of Sousse 🕓 Daily 7–7 (8–6 in winter) 👋 Moderate 🍴 Café (£) directly opposite entrance to the amphitheatre 🚌 On the main line south to Gafsa and Gabès and north to Sousse and Tunis, buses to Kairouan ❓ International Festival of Symphonic Music in July (☎ 73 630224; www.festivaleljem.com)

Archaeological museum
✉ 1km (0.5 miles) south of the amphitheatre on the road to Sfax 🕓 Daily 7–7 (8–5:30 in winter) 👋 Included in price of ticket to amphitheatre

3 Îles Kerkennah

www.kerkennah.com

The cluster of seven islands 20km (12.5 miles) off the coast of Sfax has been called 'The Last Paradise'.

Once a place of exile for the Carthaginian general Hannibal and Tunisia's former president Habib Bourguiba, there are two main inhabited islands, Chergui and Gharbi, joined together by a causeway. The islands are reached by ferry from Sfax, arriving at Sidi Youssef on the southwestern tip of the islands, with a single road running 35km (22 miles) north to the fishing village of El Attaia.

Fishing remains the main source of income for most of the 15,000 islanders. Strings of clay pots for catching squid can be seen on many quaysides, and palm fronds are used to channel fish into waiting nets. Although tourism now supplements the islands' economy, it remains very low-key. The small west coast tourist zone of Sidi Frej consists of a handful of modest hotels.

Borj el-Hissar, a ruined Aghlabid fort 3km (2 miles) north of Sidi Frej, was rebuilt by the Spanish in the 16th century; it is surrounded by Roman ruins and has the remains of several mosaics. Remla, the biggest settlement, has shops and cafés and one hotel, the Jazira. With its shallow waters and long stretches of empty sandy beaches, the island is well-suited to walking and cycling.

✚ S22 ✉ 20km (12.5 miles) east of Sfax 🍴 La Sirène (▶ 157) ⛴ Regular ferry services to Sfax from Sidi Youssef

4 Jebel Ichkeul National Park (Parc National de l'Ichkeul)

Jebel Ichkeul is one of the most important bird sanctuaries in North Africa and provides a vital stopping-off point for birds mirgating between Europe and Africa.

In 1996 the park was designated a World Heritage Site by UNESCO, but in recent years this has been dropped as dams built on its feed rivers have

caused a hige rise in the salinity of the lake water. The park authorities are keen on a rehabilitation programme to improve the lake's water level and salinity, but the future is still uncertain.

If you visit at dawn or dusk from October to February, thousands of waterfowl can be spotted on the lake. Rarer birds on the lake include the marbled teal and the purple gallinule, one of Tunisia's most colourful birds. Looking rather like an oversized moorhen, it has a bright red beak and gleaming purple-blue plumage. Sandpipers, stints and stilts are regularly found on the shores of Lac Ichkeul and Moussier's redstarts, which are indigenous to North Africa, can be spotted in the scrub. The park is also home to many animals including water buffalo, wild boar, jackals, otters and porcupines.

The park is a tranquil and uplifting place to visit at any time of the year; there are some picnic tables and several walking trails. Poppies and wild chrysanthemums bloom in the fields around the lake, and a steep climb from the car park leads to a small **Eco-Museum,** which details the area's flora and fauna and explains the ecological importance of the lake. It also has a collection of stuffed birds.

There is nowhere to stay in the park and camping is not permitted, but it makes an easy day trip from Tunis if you have your own transport.

➕ B1 ✉ 30km (18 miles) southwest of Bizerte 🕐 Daily 6am–8pm (8–6 in winter) ✋ Free 🍴 Bring your own picnic, tables provided 🚌 No public transport; access via rental car or bus to Menzel Bourguiba and then taxi

Eco-Museum
🕐 Daily 9–12, 1:30–4:30 ✋ Free

5 Kairouan

Kairouan is Tunisia's holiest city, with more than 50 mosques within the médina.

Kairouan is the fourth most important city in the Islamic world after Mecca, Medina and Jerusalem. The **Grande Mosquée de Sidi Oqba** (Great Mosque) is the star attraction here, even though non-Muslims are not allowed to enter the prayer hall with its 400 marble pillars, many of which were recovered from the ruins of Carthage and El Jem. Built in AD863, the present building is one of the most important mosques in Tunisia. Visitors can take a look through one of the 17 heavy cedar wood doors at one of the world's oldest pulpits, decorated with 250 carved wood panels. Entry may be permitted to the 128-step staircase – made from Christian tombstones – to the top of the square minaret for a superb panorama of the city.

The Mosquée des Trois Portes (Mosque of the Three Doors; closed to non-Muslims) also dates from the 9th century and features three arched doorways providing separate entrances for men, women and children.

The Zaouia de Sidi Sahab (Shrine of the Companion) on avenue de la République is the burial place of Abou Zamaa el-Balaoui, a friend of the Prophet. It is sometimes called the Barber's Mosque as el-Balaoui always wore a medallion containing three hairs from the Prophet's beard. The original mausoleum dates from the 7th century but

the tiled archways, antechambers and lovely floral mosaics were added at the end of the 17th century.

The Bassins des Aglabides (Aghlabid Pools), a short walk to the east, were part of an elaborate 9th-century water system which collected rain from the Tell Plateau via a 35km (22-mile) aqueduct.

⊞ Q19 ✉ 70km (43 miles) west of Sousse 🍴 Sabra (£), avenue de la République has good value set menus 🚌 Bus station on the main route between Tunis and Sfax via Sousse and Mahdia ❓ Mouled to celebrate the Prophet Muhammad's birthday, June

ℹ Place des Martyrs ☎ 77 231 897 🕐 Summer Mon–Sat 8–7, Sun 8–noon; winter Mon–Thu 9–1, 3–6, Fri–Sat 8:30–1. Multiple entry ticket provides access to most of the city's major attractions (available at APPC at Aghlabid Pools)

Grande Mosquée de Sidi Oqba

✉ Entrance on rue Ibrahim ibn el-Aghlab 🕐 Sun–Thu 8:30–2, Fri 8:30–noon 🖐 Part of multiple ticket (moderate)

6 Ksar Ouled Soltane

One of the enduring legacies of the Berber culture, *ksour* originally, and often still, serve as fortified grain stores.

Built from mud and stone, *ksour* (singular *ksar*) are a familiar sight in southern Tunisia, especially around Tataouine. In the hostile desert climate there might only be a good crop once every few

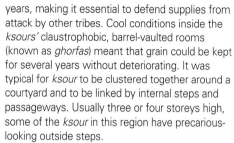

years, making it essential to defend supplies from attack by other tribes. Cool conditions inside the *ksours'* claustrophobic, barrel-vaulted rooms (known as *ghorfas*) meant that grain could be kept for several years without deteriorating. It was typical for *ksour* to be clustered together around a courtyard and to be linked by internal steps and passageways. Usually three or four storeys high, some of the *ksour* in this region have precarious-looking outside steps.

The earliest surviving *ksour* are up to 800 years old, but Ksar Ouled Soltane is among the best-known because it is particularly well preserved. Buildings in the first courtyard are more than 400 years old, while the second complex dates from around 1850. Off the beaten track, it is rarely visited and it remains a storage place for the grain and olives of the Ouled Chehida. One of the most rewarding times to visit is on Friday afternoons, when the courtyard becomes a meeting point for the local community.

A visit to Ouled Soltane is often combined with trips to other *ksour* in the area, including the 13th-century Ksar Hallouf near Zammour, part of which has been converted into a very simple hotel with primitive toilet facilities. Better accommodation and lunches are available at the 600-year-old *ksar* in Metameur, 6km (4 miles) west of Medenine.

➕ R28 ✉ 22km (14 miles) east of Tataouine 🕐 All day ✋ Free 🍴 La Médina (£), rue du 1er Juin 1955, Tatouine (☎ 75 861978) 🚌 Three buses a day from Tataouine ❓ Douirat, a very old and picturesque caravan town, is 40km (25 miles) west

7

Musée du Bardo, Tunis

Tunisia's national museum houses archaeological treasures from all over the country, but the highlight is its impressive collection of fine Roman mosaics, the largest in the world.

The Musée du Bardo is housed in a grand former palace of the Husaynid *beys* (provincial governors). It is arranged in sections covering the Carthaginian, Roman, early Christian and Islamic eras. The first rooms are dedicated to the Punic period, with stelae, masks and a priceless terracotta statue of the sun god Baal Hammon sitting on a throne, wearing a feathered headdress.

The Roman section has entire walls and floors paved with mosaics from the 2nd century BC to the 7th century AD, many almost intact. The 3rd-century mosaic of the poet Virgil writing the *Aeneid* attended by two muses, found in a villa in Sousse (➤ 132–137), and the giant *Triumph of Neptune* mosaic are among the most exceptional exhibits. Another captivating 3rd-century work

which was found at Dougga (▶ 36–37) is the mosaic of Ulysses and his sailors resisting the songs of three sirens trying to lure their vessel onto the rocks. The mosaic of Perseus rescuing Andromeda from the clutches of a sea monster was taken from an underground villa at Bulla Regia (▶ 98). Many of the smaller mosaics feature common themes, including hunting and farming scenes, Greek and Roman gods, the sea, battles and family life. Animals, birds and fish are also widely depicted.

There is also a spectacular collection of Greek bronze and marble figures, which were recovered from a Greek shipwreck found off the coast of Mahdia in the first century BC.

🞣 C3 or *Tunis b1 (off map)* ✉ Route de Bizerte, Quartier Le Bardo, 6km (4 miles) from city centre ☎ 71 513842 🕐 Tue–Sun 9–5; 9:30–4:30 in winter ✋ Moderate 🍴 Small café on ground floor (£) 🚊 Line 4 from Tunis city centre 🚌 3 from avenue Habib Bourguiba

8 Nefta

Nefta is one of the most important religious centres in Tunisia, second after Kairouan.

Legend has it that Nefta was first settled by Kostel, Noah's grandson. The oasis has a long tradition of Sufism, a mystical branch of Islam. The small oasis has more than 20 mosques and over a hundred tombs of *marabout* or local holy men (closed to non-Muslims). Many suffered severe damage after the torrential rains and floods in 1990. The Zaouia of Sidi Brahim is a complex of tombs and a *medersa* (theological school) of the Qadria, the most important Sufi brotherhood. The tomb of Marabout Sidi bou Ali is also popular, as this holy man, born in Morocco but venerated in Tunisia, is believed to have planted the first date seeds in this oasis.

In the centre of town is the place de la Libération lined with shops, and to the north is the entrance to the old quarter of the Ouled ech Cherif, with the Dar Houidi, a traditional house now turned into a museum, restaurant and bed and breakfast.

Nefta was known as the 'Princess of the Desert' until recently because of the Corbeille (French for basket), a massive crater, filled with hundreds of palm trees fed by 152 natural springs. Unfortunately the springs have dried up and water is pumped in from a large pool at the west end of the oasis, but many of the palms are dying because of drought and disease. Early evening is a good time to walk through the Corbeille, but it is advisable to do so with an official guide from the tourist office.

Nefta's main oasis covers over 10sq km (4sq miles), and has hundreds of thousands of palm

trees, which reputedly yield the best dates, the *deglet nour* (fingers of light) of the Sahara.

🕇 H15 ✉ Avenue des Sources 🕙 Daily ✋ Free 🍽 Café in the Corbeille (£), Dar Houidi (££) 🚌 Daily buses from Tunis, Tozeur, Gafsa and Kairouan to bus station on avenue Habib Bourguiba ✈ Tozeur airport 23km (14 miles) away 🛈 Avenue Habib Bourguiba 🕙 Daily 8:30–12, 2:30–5

9 Sidi Bou Saïd

Sidi Bou Saïd, perched on a cliff, is one of Tunisia's most picturesque towns. It is a popular evening hang-out for people from Tunisia and the suburbs.

The village's history goes back to the 9th century when a *ribat* (fortified monastery) was built against the Christian invaders. In the 13th century a community settled around the tomb of the holy man, Sidi bou Saïd, whose life is celebrated during a festival in August. Europeans were not allowed into the village until 1820, but the flow since then has not stopped, with visitors to the village including Gustave Flaubert who stayed here while writing *Salambo*, Paul Klee, Simone de Beauvoir and André Gide.

Many artists still live here, and though 'Sidi Bou' now attracts masses of tourists, particularly in summer, it has kept its peculiar charm. The French baron Rodolphe d'Erlanger fell in love with the village, and built a sumptuous cliffside villa here in 1912, while other wealthy French people restored houses. In 1915 the baron obtained a declaration

from the *Bey* (Governor) of Tunis to keep and protect the whitewashed architecture of the village, and to paint all the woodwork in the typical blue, one of the village's main charms today. D'Erlanger's villa, the Dar en Nejma ez Zahra, has now become a **Centre for Arab and Mediterranean Music,** with a fine collection of musical instruments and an interesting archive.

The cobbled street goes up to the main square with the wonderfully atmospheric Café des Nattes up the stairs. On the way, on the left on rue Dr Thomeur, is Dar al Annabi, a beautiful old house with 55 rooms, partially inhabited by a family, and partially by a folklore museum. Stroll though the small streets and end up at the Café Sidi Chaabane with terraces overlooking the bay.

✚ D2 ✉ 20km (12.5 miles) northeast of Tunis 🍴 Café des Nattes or Café Sidi Chaabane (➤ 109) Ⓜ TGM metro services from Tunis every 20 mins. Journey time 30 mins. 15-min uphill walk from station to centre of village ❓ Mouled of Sidi Bou Saïd in August

Centre des Musiques Arabes et Mediterranéennes
✉ Dar en Nejma ez Zahra ☎ 71 740102 🕐 Summer Tue–Sun 8:30–1, 3–6; winter Tue–Sun 9–1, 2–5 ✋ Inexpensive ❓ Concerts and performances at night

10 Thermes d'Antonin

Once the biggest Roman baths in the Empire and Carthage's best-preserved site.

The site is entered from the top of a colourful garden which slopes gently down to the sea following the pattern of the original Roman streets. Close to the entrance are the remains of a *schola*, which was a kind of after-school boys' club for the sons of wealthy Romans, with an unusual mosaic

showing children exercising. The ruins of the Byzantine Basilica of Douimes are marked by three rows of double pillars and a mosaic floor.

Visitors are not allowed to enter the baths, but can study them from a viewing platform. A white marble model shows how the baths would have looked when they were in daily use, and a couple of pillars have been repositioned to give an idea of the original height.

Work on the baths began during the reign of the Roman Emperor Hadrian (AD76–138) who spent a considerable amount of time touring his vast empire and promoting urban life. It is hard to imagine the grandeur, but to get an idea, when the public toilets were first discovered they were thought to be a theatre. Heat was provided by an underground system of furnaces and there was a series of hot rooms of varying temperatures, a cold plunge pool and a Roman-style whirlpool.

The baths are surrounded by an archaeological park with a number of Punic tombs, and the site borders the presidential palace, the official residence of the Tunisian leader, President Ben Ali.

✚ D3 ✉ Avenue des Thermes d'Antonin, Carthage
🕐 Daily 8–7 (8:30–5:30 in winter). Closed on public hols
✋ Moderate (ticket also provides entry to other Carthage ruins and the Musée National de Carthage) 🍴 Restaurant Neptune (▶ 108); several cafés on avenue Bourguiba, Carthage 🚇 Regular TGM metro services from Tunis to Carthage–Hannibal station

Best things to do

Good places to have lunch   58–59

Places to picnic   60–61

Places to take the children   62–63

Best café terraces   64–65

Top activities   66–67

A walk in the Tunis médina   68–69

Best souqs and markets   70

Best souvenirs   71

Best archaeological sites   72–73

Places to stay   74–75

Good places to have lunch

Chez Achour (££)

The best fish and seafood in town, particularly known for its fish couscous, served on the garden terrace.

✉ Rue Ali Belhouane, Hammamet ☎ 72 280140 🕐 Lunch, dinner

Dar Chakra (£–££)

Excellent Tunisian dishes served in a beautifully restored old house with a pleasant courtyard. Order specialities in advance.

✉ On left of avenue de l'Indépendance, past the Tourist Office, Monastir
☎ 73 460528 🕐 Lunch, dinner

Dar El Jeld (£££)

Superb Tunisian food in the setting of a sumptuous mansion.

✉ Rue Dar El Jeld, Tunis ☎ 71 560916 🕐 Lunch, dinner; closed Sun

La Daurade (££–£££)
Very popular fish restaurant with shaded outdoor seating.
✉ The Marina, Port El Kantaoui ☎ 73 348893 🕐 Lunch, dinner

Le Lido (££)
Sit outside opposite the harbour and enjoy fresh fish.
✉ Avenue Mohammed V, Sousse ☎ 73 225329 🕐 Lunch, dinner

Le Neptune (££)
Superb fish restaurant with a terrace on the first floor overlooking the old city and the sea.
✉ Avenue du 7-Novembre, Mahdia ☎ 73 681927 🕐 Lunch, dinner

Le Petit Mousse (££)
Delightful fish and seafood specialities are served on a shaded terrace overlooking the sea. The fish is cooked to perfection.
✉ 3.5km (2 miles) west of the centre, on the Corniche, Bizerte ☎ 72 432185 🕐 Lunch, dinner

Le Petit Navire (££)
Elegant room hidden behind a beautifully sculpted Tunisian door. Good service, as well as some of the best food in town.
✉ 123 rue de Haffouz, Sfax ☎ 74 212890 🕐 Daily noon–10pm

Restaurant Slovenia (£–££)
A wide choice of dishes, including several Tunisian specialities, prepared by one of the country's most renowned chefs, Rafik Tlati.
✉ Hôtel Les Jasmins, Nabeul ☎ 72 285343, 72 285699 🕐 Lunch,dinner

Restô (£££)
Stylish restaurant with excellent Mediterranean food and the best views over Carthage, the sea and all of Tunis.
✉ Villa Didon, next to Cathedral in Carthage ☎ 71 733433 🕐 Lunch, dinner

Places to picnic

● The empty roadside near the desert villages of Chebika, Midès and Tamerza (➤ 168, 173 and 174–175)

● Bulla Regia (➤ 98)

● Carthage (➤ 86–91)

● Dougga (➤ 36–37)

● Any of the deserted beaches on Îles Kerkennah (➤ 40–41)

● Jebel Ichkeul National Park (➤ 42–43)

● Parc du Belvédère, Tunis (➤ 84)

● Sbeïtla (➤ 151)

● Thuburbo Majus (➤ 122–123)

● Thuburnica (➤ 103)

Places to take the children

HAMMAMET
Carthageland
This theme park takes you through the history of Tunisia in an entertaining way, from the Carthaginians, Romans and Berbers to the Muslims of today. Relive the Punic Wars or cross the Alps to conquer Rome.
✉ Rue de la Médina, Yasmine Hammamet ☎ 72 240111; www.carthageland.com 🕐 All year round

Friguia Animal Park
An animal park that participates in a world programme to save endangered species, with a variety of African wildlife.
✉ Between Enfida and Bou Ficha, south of Hammamet 🕐 Summer 9–6; winter 9–4

PORT EL KANTAOUI
Acqua Palace
This waterpark is fairly modest in scale, but it offers a large swimming pool, wave machine, various waterslides and a paddling pool.

✉ 9km (5.5 miles) north of Sousse ☎ 73 348855; www.acquapalace.com
🕐 Daily 9:30–6 🍴 On-site pizzeria, self-service restaurant and bar

TUNIS
Zoo du Belvédère
This small zoo houses a selection of wild cats, birds, snakes and camels.

✉ Park Belvédère ☎ 71 281846 🕐 9–7 (9–4 in winter) 🍴 Café

Best café terraces

Café Andalous (£)
Beautifully tiled old-fashioned café.
✉ Avenue Hedi Chaker, Tabarka 🕐 7am–midnight

Café Maure (£)
Traditional café in the old stables of the kasbah.
✉ Hotel La Kasbah, Kairouan (➤ 75) ☎ 77 237301 🕐 6pm–midnight

Café Maure Diwan (£)
Atmospheric and extremely popular café on top of the médina walls.
✉ Off rue de la Kasbah, Médina, Sfax 🕐 6am–midnight

Café des Nattes (£)
See page 109.

Café de Paris (£)
See page 109.

Café Sidi Chaabane (£)
See page 109.

Café Sidi Bou Hdid (£)
See page 128.

Café Sidi Salem (£)
Several café terraces dropping down to the sea.
✉ Southside of the médina, Mahdia 🕐 8am–midnight

Dar El Medina (££–£££)
Stylish rooftop terrace with great views over the médina (➤ 74).
☎ 71 327497; www.darelmedina.com 🕐 3pm–midnight

Top activities

Bathing Many Tunisians still visit a hammam (Turkish bath) regularly. Avoid hotel hammams and go for the real thing.

Camel trekking Go for a ride in the south, or trek for several days and get away from it all.

Cycling There is no better place for bicycles than on the flat, uncrowded roads of Îles Kerkennah.

Diving Quality tuition and excellent dive sites in the waters around Tabarka.

Fishing A way of life for many Tunisians; no permit is required to fish from any of the harbours.

Four-wheel driving Ideal transport for exploring the desert region.

Golf Very high standards and eight courses to choose from.

Sailing Tunisia has some of the best marinas in North Africa. Facilities are generally of high quality and security is good. Try Bizerte, El Kantaoui, Monastir, Sidi Bou Saïd, Tabarka or Tunis (La Goulette).

Sand-skiing Using narrow skis on the sand dunes near Douz.

Water sports Try waterskiing, paragliding or windsurfing at one of the main beach resorts.

a walk

in the Tunis médina

This leisurely walk offers a good introduction to the wonderful architecture of the médina (➤ 83).

Start at the place de la Victoire, and enter the médina through the arch, and along rue Jamaa ez Zitouna until you reach the Zitouna Mosque (➤ 82). Coming out of the mosque, turn right along Souq des Libraries, with three medersas or theological schools: the Palm Tree (No 11), the Bachia (No 27) and the Slimania on the corner.

The medersas are closed but the *guardien* is always around to open them up.

Opposite is the famous Kachachine Hammam, for men only. Take the street opposite the Slimania, rue el Homsa. Opposite at No 12 rue du Trésor is Dar el Hedri, an attractive Hafsid Palace; turn left. At the end of the street, turn right on the rue des Teinturiers, past the 10th-century Ichbili Mosque, and further on the Mosquée des Teinturiers (Dyers' Mosque). Find Dar Othman (➤ 83) on the left and turn right on rue Sidi Kassem to find the excellent Dar ben Abdallah Museum (➤ 84). Continue along rue Sidi Kassem; on the right is the royal mausoleum of Tourbet el Bey (➤ 83).

The souqs are always lively, particularly in the morning and late afternoon.

Turn right on rue Tourbet Bey and continue along the Souq des Femmes into Souq des Étoffes (Fabric Souq). Past the Zitouna Mosque turn right on Souq el Attarine, and immediately left on Sidi ben Arous. In the alleys to the left is the Souq des Chechias; turn left on rue de la Kasbah to reach the place du Gouvernement, with the imposing Dar el Bey, now the prime minister's office.

Distance 1.5–2km (1–1.2 miles)
Time 3–4 hours allowing for visits and shopping
Start point Place de la Victoire ✚ *Tunis d3*
End point Place du Gouvernement ✚ *Tunis b4*
Lunch Dar El Jeld (➤ 58), Dar El Medina (➤ 74)

Best souqs and markets

Houmt Souq
Great for jewellery, especially the 'hands of Fatima' (see opposite), carpets and leatherware.

Kairouan
The Centre des Traditions et des Métiers d'Art de Kairouan is the best place to buy woven and hand-knotted carpets.

Nabeul
Attractive covered souq overlooked by the domes and white walls of the Grande Mosquée. Nabeul is famous for its pottery.

Sousse
Famous Sunday market at Souq el-Ahad, where you can buy everything from camels to computers.

Tunis
Especially off rue Jemaa ez Zitouna – a fascinating area of winding alleys, with jewellery, clothing and crafts.

Best souvenirs

Carpets
While not cheap, they will make a handsome and long-lasting souvenir and are readily available all over Tunisia, particularly in Tunis, El Jem, Sfax and Kairouan – the King of the Carpet Centres. Make sure any carpet you purchase has a label of authenticity attached.

Food
If you like couscous, bring back a *couscoussier*, which is also handy to steam vegetables. Mint tea is good for you, so look for the cheap blue teapots. Sahel olives and Tunisian dates are excellent, as is the Tunisian *harissa* (chilli sauce). No one can resist the delicious marzipan sweets available from Tunisian patisseries.

Jewellery
Houmt Souq in Jerba is one of the best places for silver and gold pieces. Common motifs include fishes and the Hand of Fatima, to protect the wearer against the evil eye. Big, chunky Berber jewellery can also be found in Jerba and Tunis.

Pottery
Best buys include plates, bowls, vases and tiles, which, if you buy several, can make a very attractive wall panel. The two big production centres are Guellala on the island of Jerba, and Nabeul.

Woodwork and metalwork
The best wood carving is to be found in Sfax where olive wood is turned into bowls, spoons and chess boards. The tapping of hammers and chisels on brass is a familiar sound in any of the souqs where ashtrays, plates and trays are among the most popular items. Craftsman will often offer to engrave a name on pieces bought.

Best archaeological sites

Bulla Regia Amazing Roman site with underground villas and beautiful, well-preserved mosaics (➤ 98).

Carthage The overgrown ruins of what was once the largest city in Africa (➤ 86–91).

Dougga The most spectacular Roman site in Tunisia (➤ 36–37).

El Jem Gigantic Roman amphitheatre that could accommodate 15,000 spectators (➤ 38–39).

Kerkouane No one destroyed this ancient Punic town, instead time took its toll (➤ 117).

Matmata Underground troglodytic dwellings, and the set for *Star Wars* (➤ 172).

Sbeïtla The most southerly of the Roman cities, with the best-preserved Forum temple complex (➤ 151).

Thermes d'Antonin Massive Roman baths complex at Carthage (➤ 54–55).

Thuburbo Majus
Only a fraction of the Roman city has been excavated. Buildings include a capitol, forum temples, baths and villas (➤ 122–123).

Utique (Utica)
Before Carthage, this was the first Phoenician trading post in North Africa (➤ 103).

Places to stay

Claridge (£)
Once the most superior place in town, but now overshadowed by the beach hotels along the corniche. In a central location between the médina and the beach. The large comfortable rooms all have a bath or shower – but not all have en-suite toilets.

✉ 10 avenue Habib Bourguiba, Sousse ☎ 73 224759

Dar Faïza (£)
Simple but comfortable hotel set in the old villa of a French count, just outside the centre of Houmt Souq. The rooms overlook the lush bougainvillaea gardens with a swimming pool.

✉ 6 rue de la République, opposite the Borj el-Kebir, Jerba ☎ 75 650083; www.darfaizadarsalem.com

Dar Hayet (££–£££)
The smallest and most discreet of Hammamet's deluxe hotels. Rooms are all doubles and are plushly decorated with locally produced furnishings; most have sea views.

✉ Rue de la Corniche, Hammamet ☎ 72 282856

Dar El Medina (££–£££)
The first hotel in the médina, in a fabulous and grand old house, now turned into a small luxury hotel. The decoration and eye for detail is wonderful, but kept totally in line with the traditional médina architecture.

✉ 64 rue Sidi ben Arous, Tunis ☎ 71 563022; www.darelmedina.com

Dar Saïd (££–£££)
Charming hotel in a restored 19th-century house in the heart of Sidi Bou Saïd, set around four patios with fountains and running water. There is a small swimming pool in the peaceful garden with century-old cypresses, overlooking the Mediterranean.

✉ Rue Toumi, Sidi Bou Saïd ☎ 71 729666; www.darsaid.com.tn

Marhala (£)

This converted underground house is run by the Touring Club de Tunisie. Popular, so book well ahead.

✉ Off Toujane road, Matmata ☎ 75 240015

La Kasbah (££)

Built like a kasbah, this is the best hotel in Kairouan, with a great pool in the courtyard and several restaurants.

✉ Avenue Ibn el-Jazzar, Kairouan ☎ 77 237301; www.goldenjasmin.com/la-kasbah

Les Mimosas (££)

Moorish-style hotel in an old palace on a hill, with fantastic views over the mountain, town, marina and sea.

✉ On the road above the petrol station at the entrance to Tabarka

☎ 78 673018; 78 673028; www.hotel-les-mimosas.com

La Résidence (£££)

One of Tunisia's newest and most luxurious hotels with a thalassotherapy spa, tennis courts, Mediterranean restaurant and free shuttle service to Tunis city centre.

✉ 2km (1.2 miles) north of Gammarth ☎ 71 910101; www.theresidence-tunis.com

Tamerza Palace Hotel (££–£££)

Stylish, well-run hotel overlooking the ruined village of Tamerza. A good base for exploring the desert region.

✉ Tamerza ☎ 76 485344; www.tamerza-palace.com

Exploring

Tunis and the North	79–110
Cap Bon	111–130
Central Tunisia	131–158
Jerba and the South	159–186

For a small country, Tunisia offers plenty of variety besides its glorious beaches. The north, particularly around Aïn Draham, has large oak forests and lakes, making it feel more like Europe than Africa. The Sahara desert covers nearly the whole south of Tunisia, with huge dunes and shifting sands. The relentlessly barren landscape of the Grand Erg Oriental is accessible only by four-wheel-drive vehicles, and even then only with guides and several other vehicles in tow. Also in the south are two great *chotts* (salt lakes) – Chott el Jerid and Chott el Gharsa.

Apart from a few Phoenician settlements, most of the archaeological sites are Roman. The cities often have a well-preserved médina (old walled city), built after the Arabs came to North Africa to spread Islam. The modern towns grew around these médinas, and usually have a number of beautiful colonial buildings.

Tunis and the North

Although northern Tunisia is home to over a quarter of the population, most visitors bypass this area altogether and head straight for the east coast beach resorts. This is a pity as the capital – Tunis – is here, and the surrounding countryside and coastline are enormously varied.

Tunis

Tunis has more than enough attractions to warrant a few nights' stay or, at the very least, a full day's excursion. For more than 3,000 years, Tunis has been among the great cities of the Mediterranean and it has plenty of monuments to show for it. It is also a convenient base for independent travellers, with dozens of quiet beaches and some of the country's finest archaeological sites within easy reach.

Tabarka is slowly emerging as Tunisia's northern flagship resort, while the charming old port town of Bizerte is still debating whether it really wants to entice international tourists or is quite content to remain a sleepy backwater.

TUNIS

Tunis started life as a small garrison town, defended by the high walls of its médina. Its expansion into a wealthy trading city was sparked by the Arab invasion of Tunisia in the 7th century, though it was another 600 years before Tunis became the capital.

Today the city is the undisputed focal point of the nation. It is home to one in ten of the population and forms the epicentre of political, cultural and social life. The city combines a vibrant, atmospheric old town of narrow lanes and covered souqs with the more European-style Ville Nouvelle, characterized by tree-lined avenues and elegant colonnaded, balconied buildings.
www.tourismtunisia.com

✈ D3 ✉ 66km
(41 miles) southeast
of Bizerte
🛈 1 avenue Mohamed V
☎ 71 341077
🕐 Mon–Sat 8–6,
Sun 9–noon

Avenue Habib Bourguiba

The 'Champs Élysées' of Tunis, avenue Habib Bourguiba is the capital's best-known and most prestigious thoroughfare, where seemingly the whole of the city comes for a late afternoon coffee.

Apart from a few grand buildings there is a mishmash of banks, *bureaux de change*, patisseries, cinemas, car rental agents and hotels, including Hotel Africa – the most prominent landmark and a popular meeting place (➤ 107).

Avenue Habib Bourguiba begins at the foot of avenue de France, close to the main entrance to the médina. Where the streets run together is the **Cathédrale de St Vincente de Paul,** a Catholic church built in 1882. Just across the road is the Ambassade de France (French Embassy) from where the Protectorate was governed between 1881 and independence was granted in 1956. Further east is the art nouveau French Théâtre Municipal, which regularly features good Arabic and classical music concerts.

✚ *Tunis g3* 🍴 Café at Hotel Africa (➤ 107), Chez Nous (➤ 110) 🚌 5, 8, 35, 50 🚇 Line 1, Tunis Marine

Cathédrale de St Vincente de Paul

✚ *Tunis f3* ✉ Avenue Habib Bourguiba 🕐 Daily service at 6:30pm and Sundays at 9 and 11am ✋ Free (donations accepted)

Jemaa ez Zitouna

Jemaa ez Zitouna (the Great Mosque) covers an area of more than 5,000sq m (53,820sq ft) and is the largest mosque in Tunis, dwarfing the surrounding alleyways. It has been at the spiritual heart of Tunis for over 1,000 years and is the only mosque in the city which can be visited by non-Muslims, though access is restricted to a viewing enclosure overlooking the polished marble courtyard.

Jemaa ez Zitouna (literally Mosque of the Olive Tree) dates mostly from the middle of the 9th century, though it has been modified many times since, and was inspired by the slightly larger Grande Mosquée de Sidi Oqba (Great Mosque) in Kairouan (➤ 44). Its outer wall is built of stone taken from Roman Carthage. The courtyard is flanked on three sides by simple arcades and on the fourth by a prayer hall supported by 184 columns.

During the 13th and 14th centuries the mosque became an important Islamic university attracting students from all over the Arab world. It continued to flourish until the 1950s when the teaching faculty was closed on the orders of President Bourguiba in a bid to reduce religious influence in the country. The mosque and its 500-year-old library, containing one of the world's greatest collections of Arab literature, had its teaching status restored in 1987 by President Ben Ali.

Tunis c4 Rue Jemaa ez Zitouna 8–2:30. Closed Fri Inexpensive Café ez Zitouna (£), rue Jemaa ez Zitouna 1 Habib Thameur

Médina

The medieval part of Tunis is a UNESCO World Heritage Site. It dates back to the 7th century and remained the commercial centre until the establishment of the French Protectorate in 1881, after which it began to decline. Start by exploring the narrow alleys at the **Bab el Bahr** (also known as the Sea Gate or Porte de France) on place de la Victoire.

The **Mosquée de Hammouda Pacha** with its thin Turkish-style minaret, and the **Mosquée Sidi Youssef** with an octagonal minaret, the oldest of its type in the city, are closed to non-Muslims. There is a good view of Sidi Youssef from the rooftop of the Musée des Turcs, an antiques shop in Souq et Trouk. **Dar Othman** (courtyard open; free) was a palace built for Othman Dey, who ruled Tunisia from 1598 to 1610 (➤ 69). The rue des Libraires contains three small 18th-century *medersas* (theological schools) at Nos 11 and 27 and on the corner of the street. **Tourbet el Bey** in rue Tourbet el Bey is a royal mausoleum built in the late 18th century for the Husaynid princes.

✚ *Tunis c3*

Bab el Bahr
✉ Place de la Victoire

Mosquée de Hammouda Pacha
✉ Just off rue Sidi Ben Arous

Mosquée Sidi Youssef
✉ Near Souq el Berka

Dar Othman
✉ Rue el M'Bazaa

Tourbet el Bey
✉ Rue Tourbet el Bey ⊙ Daily 9:30–4:30
👊 Inexpensive

Musée des Arts Populaires et Traditions

The Museum of Popular Arts and Traditions occupies a late 18th-century palace, the Dar Ben Abdallah. The ornate entrance leads into a marble courtyard with a fountain, showing the visitor a tantalizing example of the largely hidden side of the old city. In many ways the building itself is more interesting than the exhibition rooms, which show upper class urban life in Tunis in the 19th century.

➕ *Tunis d5* ✉ Impasse Ben Abdallah, off rue Sidi Kacem ☎ 71 256195 🕐 Mon–Sat 9:30–4:30 ✋ Inexpensive 🍴 Plenty of choice 🚌 1 🚇 Place Barcelone

Musée du Bardo

Best places to see, ➤ 48–49.

Parc du Belvédère

The Belvedere Park was laid out by the French as an exclusive enclave for the families of the ruling classes. Today, with so few green open spaces in the city, the park is a popular place to escape the summer heat. An elegant 18th-century pavilion (or *koubba*) is half-way up the hill and from the top there is a good view of the city. There is also a small **zoo** (➤ 63).

➕ *Tunis f1 (off map)* ✉ Avenue Taïeb Mehiri 🕐 Open access but avoid at night ✋ Free 🍴 Couple of cafés serving drinks 🚌 5, 5c, 5d 🚇 Palestine ❓ Concerts in summer

Zoo

🕐 9–7 (to 4 in winter) ✋ Inexpensive 🍴 Café

Souqs

Shopping in the souqs (markets) is one of the biggest attractions of the médina for many. The myriad tiny alleys provide endless opportunities for finding Tunisian crafts. Originally each souq specialized in a single trade, though many now sell souvenirs often made in China. Among the oldest is the 13th-century Souq el Attarine (the perfume-makers' market), which still sells scents and essential oils. The Souq des Etoffes sells fabric and traditional clothes; search out the Souq du Cuivre for copper items, the Souq des Babouches for leather slippers, and the Souq el Kebabjia for silk. The Souq et Trouk (market of the Turks) was one of the city's finest when it opened in 1630, and the Souq el Berka was one of the largest slave markets in the Mediterranean.

✚ *Tunis c4* ✉ Throughout the médina 🕐 Mostly closed on Sun 🍴 M'Rabet Café (£), Souq et Trouk 🚌 1 🚇 Habib Thameur

CARTHAGE

The city of Carthage was a place of grandeur and power, and it inspired several legends, from its foundation by Queen Dido to her doomed romance with the Roman Aeneas. You need a lot of imagination to bring it back to life, as the Phoenician town was utterly destroyed by the Romans, and later by the Vandals, and the few remains are scattered over a large area in a residential suburb.

Founded in 814BC by the Phoenicians, by the fourth century BC Carthage had become the centre of their vast maritime empire. In 146BC it was destroyed by the Romans who – only 25 years later – began rebuilding on the same site. It became the third largest city of the Roman Empire before it was destroyed first by the Vandals, and then by the Arabs in AD692, ending its heyday.

✚ D3 ✉ 15–20km (9–12.5 miles) northeast of Tunis 🕗 8–7 in summer; daily 8:30–5:30 in winter ✋ Multiple-entry ticket to all the monuments in Carthage 🍴 Restaurant Neptune (££) and Restô (▶ 59) 🚊 TGM every 20 mins, stopping at six stations in Carthage: Salammbo, Byrsa, Dermech,

Hannibal, Presidential and Amilcar 🔲 Carthage International Festival
Jul–Aug; www.festival-carthage.com.tn

Byrsa Hill

It is possible to see the whole of the site from the summit of
Byrsa Hill. This was
the spiritual heart of
the city under Punic
rule and is the best
place to start a tour.
The **Cathédrale de
St Louis** built here in
1890 is dedicated to
the French king who
died in 1279 while
trying to lay siege to
Tunis. The cathedral
has been restored as a

cultural centre for Arab music and is now known as the
Acropolium. The Musée National de Carthage (➤ 89) is worth
a visit for an overview of the site and to see some of the
magnificent treasures dating back to the city's earliest days.
🚉 Carthage–Hannibal

Cathédrale de St Louis

✉ Byrsa Hill 🔲 Concerts are held here throughout the year; music festival
in October; www.acropolium.com.tn

Cimetière

The American War Cemetery commemorates the 6,564
Americans who died in North Africa during World War II. There are
2,840 neatly tended graves and a Wall of Remembrance naming
those who were never found.
✉ Rue Roosevelt 🚉 Carthage–Presidential

Les Ports Puniques

In the second century the twin Punic Ports provided berths for more than 200 naval ships, but today it is almost impossible to imagine such a sight. The southern commercial port was linked to the other military port by a narrow channel. You can just see the shape of these once ingenious harbours, but the **Musée des Ports Puniques** has fascinating reconstructions of both Phoenician and Roman ports. It shows them as one giant shipyard surrounded by several slipways. The nearby **Musée Océanographique** (Oceanographic Museum) has been modernized, with some interactive displays bringing a bit of life to an otherwise dull collection of fish and nauticalia.

✉ Rue Hannibal 🚊 Carthage–Salammbo

Musée des Ports Puniques

✉ Îlot de l'Amirante 🕐 8:30–5; 7pm in summer ✋ Free

Musée Océanographique

✉ Avenue 2 Mars ☎ 71 730420 🕐 Tue–Sat 10–1, 3–6, Sun 10–6 ✋ Inexpensive

Musée National de Carthage

The National Museum of Carthage houses collections of sculpture, statues, masks and mosaics. On the ground floor are Carthaginian, Roman and Christian remains, while the first floor has incense burners and plates found inside Punic graves, as well as glass, ceramics and amphorae.

☎ 71 730036 ✉ Near the cathedral ③ Summer daily 8–7 (8:30–5 in winter). Undergoing restoration ✋ Moderate ⊙ Carthage–Dermech or Carthage–Hannibal

Musée Romain et Paléo-Chrétien

The small Roman and Palaeo-Christian Museum is located at the crossroads of two ancient Roman streets over a still-intact Roman cistern. Excavations are ongoing and exhibits include two peacock mosaics and a 5th-century marble statue of Ganymede, cupbearer of the gods.

③ Summer daily 9–7 (9–5 in winter) ✋ Inexpensive ⊙ Carthage–Dermech

Quartier Magon

Located close to the Thermes d'Antonin (➤ 54–55), the Magon Quarter has been turned into an archaeological park. There are two small exhibition rooms and a display of mosaic pavements.

✉ Avenue de la République 🚋 Carthage–Hannibal

Sanctuary of Tophet

It is hard to imagine this quiet, overgrown garden was used for child sacrifice. Excavations have unearthed more than 20,000 urns containing the ashes of boys aged between two and twelve, sacrificed by Carthaginians in the 8th century BC. The remains were cremated as an offering to the sun god, Baal Hammon, and the moon goddess, Tanit.

✉ Avenue Farhat Hached 🕒 Daily 9–7 (9–5 in winter) 🖐 Inexpensive
🚋 Carthage–Salammbo

Théâtre d'Hadrien

There is little or nothing left of the original Theatre of Hadrian built in the early 2nd century, but it has now been completely restored and is very popular as a venue for concerts and plays during the

annual Carthage International Festival. Just beyond the theatre is the Parc Archéologique des Villas Romaines (Archaeological Park of Roman Villas), a collection of columns, statues and a few mosaics – but best known for its views over the Bay of Tunis.

✉ Avenue 7 Novembre 🖐 Inexpensive
🚋 Carthage–Hannibal ❓ Carthage International Festival in the summer; www.festival-carthage.com.tn

Thermes d'Antonin

Best places to see, ➤ 54–55.

More to see around Tunis

GAMMARTH

Once a quiet seaside village, Gammarth is now a wealthy suburb of
greater Tunis, with several expensive hotels and restaurants on the
coast. In the 1950s the beaches gained notoriety for attracting
European nudists and became known locally as the Baies des
Singes (Bay of Monkeys). Raoued Plage, beyond Gammarth, is a
fine stretch of sand and is packed with families during the summer
months. Above the beaches, on the Hauts de Gammarth, is Jebel
Khawi (Hollow Mountain), where there is a French military
cemetery for more than 4,000 Frenchmen killed during World War II.

✚ D2 ✉ 20km (12.5 miles) northeast of Tunis 🍴 Good choice (£–£££)
🚌 20b from Jardin Thameur in Tunis city centre

LA GOULETTE

Despite its rundown houses, crumbling kasbah and air of neglect,
La Goulette is popular for its fish restaurants attracting crowds
from the city on summer weekends. Once a pirates' stronghold

and home to a large Jewish community, La Goulette ('the gullet') is at the mouth of the Tunis canal and is still a major cargo and ferry port. The kasbah, built in 1535, was used as a dungeon for prisoners waiting to be taken to Tunis to be sold as slaves.

✚ D3 ✉ 15km (9 miles) northeast of Tunis 🍴 Café Vert, 68 avenue Franklin D. Roosevelt (££–£££) ✉ Place 7 Novembre ☎ 71 737310 🚊 TGM from Tunis Marine ✈ Tunis–Carthage Airport 10km (6 miles)

LA MARSA

La Marsa is a trendy beachfront suburb on the Bay of Tunis. With a palm tree-lined corniche and a long sandy beach, it is a popular weekend destination for residents of Tunis and a permanent home for the well-heeled. Two of the town's finest residences belong to the ambassadors of Britain and France.

✚ D2 ✉ 15km (9 miles) northeast of Tunis 🍴 Several (££–£££) around the metro station 🚊 Regular TGM from Tunis ✈ Airport 12km (7.5 miles)

SIDI BOU SAÏD

Best places to see, ➤ 52–53.

More to see in the North

BÉJA

Formerly a Roman garrison, the town was destroyed by the Vandals in the 5th century and again in the 10th and 11th centuries. Since then it has become an important agricultural centre.

The fertile land attracted many Europeans, who left their mark in the form of large, colonial buildings. The médina, although a bit run-down, is very atmospheric. Locally handwoven blankets are sold in Souq en Nehasah, and rue el Attarine is the food and spice market. The Byzantine kasbah is used by the military and is not open to the public. There are Colonial and Commonwealth war cemeteries out beyond the station.

🚹 L6 ✉ 110km (68 miles) west of Tunis 🍴 Restaurant at Hôtel Phénix (££), 8 avenue de la République ☎ 78 450188 🚃 Daily trains from Tunis
🚌 Frequent services from Tunis

BIZERTE

Bizerte is the largest town on the north coast, with a picturesque old port and bustling médina. It has slowly begun to embrace tourism, with the building of several hotels along the route de la Corniche, but it is easily visited on a day trip from Tunis, less than an hour's drive away.

Bizerte has been a major port since the Phoenicians built a canal linking the inland Lac de Bizerte (Lake Bizerte) with the open sea, creating one of the finest harbours in the western Mediterranean. Known then as Hippo Zarytus, it was renamed Bizerte in 678 after being captured by the Arabs. In the 16th century – under Turkish rule – Bizerte became a pirates' den. The French made it their principal naval base in the late 19th century and it has remained a military centre, with young men in uniform a common sight on the town's streets.

The Vieux Port (Old Port), surrounded by shops and café terraces and dotted with colourful fishing boats, is the heart of the town. At the mouth of the harbour is the **kasbah,** which, despite its Byzantine appearance, dates mainly from the 17th century. In places the walls are up to 10m (33ft) high and 11m (36ft) thick, and within is a maze of narrow, winding passageways. Facing the kasbah is the smaller Sidi el Hani fortress, which has been turned into a small but dull **Musée Océanographique** (Oceanographic Museum), featuring a motley collection of local fish.

West of the kasbah is the médina, which was heavily bombed during World War II. Closed to non-Muslims, the 17th-century Grande Mosquée (Great Mosque) with its octagonal minaret is best viewed from rue des Armuriers in the street behind or, better still, from the opposite side of the harbour. The **Zaouia de Sidi Mokhtar** houses the local branch of the Association de Sauvegarde de la Médina, which seeks to preserve and restore the area. Displays include a map of the town showing how it looked in 1881. North of the médina the **Fort d'Espagne** (Spanish Fort, which was actually built by the Turks in the 1570s) offers an excellent view over Bizerte. The main beach runs for 5km (3 miles) alongside the route de la Corniche to Cap Bizerte.

✚ C1 ✉ 66km (41 miles) northwest of Tunis 🍴 Le Petit Mousse (➤ 59) 🚉 Station on rue de Russie 🚌 To Tunis every half hour from Quai Tarik Ibn Zaid ℹ️ At the old harbour ☎ 72 432897

Kasbah
✉ North of the Old Harbour 🕐 Tue–Sun 9–12:30, 3–7; in summer daily 9–12:30, 4–midnight ✋ Inexpensive

Musée Océanographique
✉ Avenue Habib Bourguiba
🕐 Tue–Sun 9–12:30, 3–7
✋ Inexpensive

Zaouia de Sidi Mokhtar
✉ Place Lahedine Bouchoucha
🕐 Exhibitions ✋ Free

Fort d'Espagne
✉ Boulevard Hassan en Nouri ✋ Free

BULLA REGIA

This Roman site is as remarkable as Dougga but, being off the beaten track, it is never overrun with visitors, making it much more atmospheric. Neolithic tombs at the site suggest Bulla Regia was inhabited long before the Romans and it was certainly the capital of one of the short-lived Numidian kingdoms. After it was annexed by Emperor Hadrian in the 2nd century it became one of the wealthiest Roman cities in North Africa.

The rich wheat and olive merchants of the town used to escape the summer heat by retreating to underground villas. Many were paved with beautiful mosaics and although some of the best have been moved to the Musée du Bardo in Tunis (➤ 48–49), others remain here, undisturbed for centuries. These include the mosaic of Venus and a cupid riding on dolphins at the Maison d'Amphitrite (House of Amphitrite); and a mosaic of fishermen at the Maison de la Pêche (House of Fishing), the oldest surviving villa. La Maison de la Chasse (House of the Hunt) has an elegant colonnaded courtyard and a sophisticated private baths complex.

Bulla Regia's two most impressive public buildings are a small, beautifully preserved theatre, and the Memmian Baths close to the site entrance. The market square and forum are flanked by the ruins of two temples to Isis and Apollo, whose priceless collection of statues are also now at the Musée du Bardo. A small museum is at the entrance to the site.

✚ K6 ✉ 60km (37 miles) south of Tabarka; 7km (4 miles) northwest of Jendouba ⏰ Daily 8–7 (8:30–5:30 in winter) ✋ Inexpensive 🍴 Cafés and restaurants at Jendouba 🚌 To Jendouba from Tunis or Bizerte, then taxi or *louage* (shared taxi)

DOUGGA

Best places to see, ➤ 36–37.

JEBEL ICHKEUL NATIONAL PARK
Best places to see, ➤ 42–43.

TABARKA
Tabarka is Tunisia's flagship resort on the north coast. During the late 1980s and early 1990s the Tunisian government invested heavily in the town, building a marina, an 18-hole golf course and an international airport nearby. It's used mainly in summer, bringing in Tunisian, German and Italian visitors.

Nestled beneath the Kroumirie Mountains, which are still covered with cork oaks, pine and eucalyptus, the small fishing village is not without charm, offering a long, unspoiled stretch of sandy beach to the east of the centre and a series of small rocky coves to the west. The area is developing a reputation as a watersports centre with quality facilities for sailing, diving and windsurfing. Tunnels Reef (20 minutes by boat from Tabarka) is an extraordinary complex of tunnels, caves, caverns and gullies.

The town began life as a Phoenician settlement and prospered in Roman times as a trading port for the export of marble from the quarries in Chemtou. In 1541 the Turkish pirate Barbarossa gave Tabarka to Charles V of Spain in exchange for his pirate comrade Dragut. Modern-day Tabarka was largely designed by the French, who also built the causeway connecting the island of Tabarka to the mainland. In 1952 Habib Bourguiba, who later became president, was exiled to Tabarka by the French.

The focal point of the town is avenue Habib Bourguiba, where most of the shops and restaurants are to be found. Many shops sells cork products, and Mediterranean coral, now listed as an endangered species. The old port has been expanded into a luxury marina, Porto Corallo, and across the water is a 16th-century Genoese fort.

Les Aiguilles (The Needles), at the western end of the coastal road, are 20m-high (65ft) rock formations sculpted by erosion. They are a popular meeting point for the local youths at the end of the afternoon.

✚ K5 ✉ 175km (110 miles) from Tunis ▮▮ Touta (➤ 109) 🚌 Up to six buses daily to Tunis ✈ Tabarka Airport, 14km (8.5 miles) east of town
ℹ Avenue du 7-Novembre 1987 ☎ 78 673555 🕐 Mon–Sat 8:30–1, 3–5:45 (8–8 in summer)

THUBURNICA

Way out west, only 15km (9 miles) from the Algerian border, the Roman remains at Thuburnica are not exceptional, but the scenery is very impressive.

The most intact remnant of the town is the beautiful Roman bridge crossing the bed of a river which carries the run-off from the surrounding hills in winter. This bridge is still used to reach the ruins of the town itself. Visitors who know what they are looking for will see the remains of a couple of temples, a triumphal arch and parts of a two-storey mausoleum. At the top of the hill is a small Byzantine fort.

✚ K6 ✉ 180km (112 miles) west of Tunis ☻ Open access ✋ Free
🍴 Small cafés at Ghardimaou 🚃 To Ghardimaou and then taxi

UTIQUE (UTICA)

Halfway between Tunis and Bizerte is Utique, now 10km (6 miles) from the sea, though in Roman times it was an important port and the capital of the province of Africa. Much of the old Roman city lies buried under the deep mud of the Oued Mejerda (Mejerda River), which has been silting up for the past thousand years. The most intact part of the Roman remains is around the Maison de la Cascade (House of the Waterfall), which belonged to a very wealthy private citizen. The fountain in the courtyard, which gave its name to the house, still has remarkable mosaics.

The ruins of Utica's once-massive public baths complex still give an idea of how impressive they must once have been. Just in front of the entrance to the site there is a small museum containing pottery and other objects found during the excavation of the baths.

✚ C2 ✉ 30km (18.5 miles) southeast of Bizerte ☻ Daily 8–7 (8:30–5:30 in winter) ✋ Inexpensive 🍴 Picnic tables provided 🚌 Regular bus services between Tunis and Bizerte; get off at the turning about 2km (1.2 miles) from the site

a drive from Tunis to Lac Ichkeul

**An absorbing full-day itinerary combining a
peaceful nature reserve, Roman ruins and one
of the most atmospheric towns in the country.**

*Head northwest out of Tunis on the Tabarka road (7),
through Jedeida to Mateur. Turn right towards Tinja and
Menzel Bourguiba, following the signs to Lac Ichkeul.*

The road becomes a track near the entrance to the park
and at the gate visitors are asked to sign an official form (in
French) promising to treat the countryside with respect.

*From the gate, it is another 3km (2 miles) to the car park
for the Eco-Museum (➤ 43) and the starting point for
various walks. Leave the park following signs for Bizerte.
After 15km (9 miles), take the turning to Menzel
Bourguiba, the former French garrison town of Ferryville.*

The town was founded at the
end of the 19th century to house
European immigrants. Once
nicknamed 'Little Paris', it has
lost much of its charm but is
worth a short stop on the way.

*Return to the main
Mateur–Bizerte road at
the village of Tinja.*

Fishermen can usually be seen
battling to stop eel and mullet
finding a way through the mesh
of nets from Jebel Ichkeul to the
open sea.

Head 20km (12.5 miles) north to Bizerte (➤ 96–97), the largest town on the north coast. Leave Bizerte on the Tunis road (8). After 30km (18.5 miles), there is a sign to the old Roman city of Utique (➤ 103). From Utique it is another 30km (18.5 miles) back to the centre of Tunis.

Distance 180km (112 miles)
Time 8 hours, including several stops
Start/end point Tunis ✚ D3
Lunch Le Petit Mousse (➤ 59)

HOTELS

BIZERTE
Bizerta Resort (£££)
Four-star beachfront hotel in the *Zone Touristique* with indoor and outdoor swimming pools and a health club. The comfortable bedrooms are equipped with minibars and satellite television.
✉ Route de la Corniche ☎ 72 436966; www.bizertaresort.com

Le Petit Mousse (££)
Well-run hotel with an excellent restaurant (➤ 59). The only negative feature is that the private beach is just a very narrow strip, close to the road.
✉ Route de la Corniche (6km/4 miles from the centre) ☎ 72 432185

CARTHAGE
Villa Didon (£££)
The modern Villa Didon is furnished by ultra-hip designers like Ron Arad and Phillipe Starck and displays contemporary artwork by North African artists such as Rachid Koraichi. The large rooms are sumptuous and have superb views of the Bay of Tunis and Carthage. Excellent restaurant and spa.
✉ Byrsa Hill ☎ 71 733433; www.villadidon.com

GAMMARTH
La Résidence (£££)
See page 75.

SIDI BOU SAÏD
Dar Saïd (££–£££)
See page 74.

Sidi Bou Saïd (££)
This small hotel is owned by the Tunisian National Tourist Office to provide hands-on experience for students at the adjacent hotel school. Full of character, it has a swimming pool, tennis courts and – from its sun terrace – an excellent view of Tunis.
✉ Avenue Sidi Dhrif (800m/half a mile north of the village) ☎ 71 740411

TABARKA
Abou Nawas Montazah (£££)
This sprawling beachfront hotel has tennis courts and a diving centre, but the rooms can be very noisy.

✉ Route Touristique ☎ 78 673532; www.abounawas.com

Les Mimosas (££)
See page 75.

TUNIS
Carlton (££)
A clean mid-market hotel, offering great value and comfortable rooms with TV and en-suite bathrooms. Very friendly staff and good central location.

✉ 31 avenue Habib Bourguiba ☎ 71 330644; www.hotelcarltontunis.com

Dar El Medina (££–£££)
See page 74.

Excel (££)
A central, clean and comfortable hotel, offering in-room television and telephone and a friendly bar, next door to the Carlton.

✉ 35 avenue Habib Bourguiba ☎ 71 355088; www.hotelexcel.com

Hotel Africa (££–£££)
One of the city's major landmarks, the Africa fronts the bustling main thoroughfare. The spacious rooms with great views over the city have been renovated, but are still aimed mostly at business travellers. The terrace is great for a coffee or a snack.

✉ 50 avenue Habib Bourguiba ☎ 71 347477; www.elmouradi.com

Hotel de la Médina (£)
Probably the most pleasant of the budget médina hotels, with clean double rooms; however, there are no singles or en-suite facilities.

✉ Place de la Victoire ☎ 71 327497

Hotel de Russie (£££)

Spotless hotel discreetly located in a back street just off the bustling rue el Jazira.

✉ 18 rue de Russie ☎ 71 328883

Maison Dorée (£–££)

A well-maintained budget hotel with the atmosphere of a bygone age and somewhat formal staff. Ask for a room at the front of the hotel, which is quieter.

✉ 6 rue de Hollande (entrance in rue el Koufa) ☎ 71 240631

Transatlantique (£)

Another fairly basic hotel with large and noisy bedrooms, but attractively tiled lobby and passageways.

✉ 106 rue de Yougoslavie ☎ 71 240680

RESTAURANTS

BIZERTE

Le Petit Mousse (££)

See page 59.

Le Sport Nautique (£££)

Ideal for a leisurely lunch overlooking the entrance to the harbour.

✉ Boulevard Habib Bourguiba ☎ 72 432262 🕔 Lunch, dinner; closed during Ramadan

CARTHAGE

Restaurant Neptune (££)

This simple but delightful Mediterranean fish restaurant has a large terrace overlooking the sea and a few of Carthage's ruins sunk into it. Perfectly cooked fish and seafood.

✉ Waterfront in Quartier Magon ☎ 71 731456 🕔 Lunch, dinner

Restô (£££)

See page 59.

LA GOULETTE
Le Café Vert (££)
The leader among the cluster of mid- to upmarket fish restaurants. *Poisson Complet* is the most requested dish.

✉ 68 avenue Franklin Roosevelt ☎ 71 736156 🕐 Lunch, dinner; closed Mon

SIDI BOU SAÏD
Au Bon Vieux Temps (££–£££)
Succulent French and Tunisian dishes are served here. Book ahead.

✉ 56 rue Heidi Chaker ☎ 71 744733 🕐 Noon–midnight

Café des Nattes (£)
Linger and relax while enjoying a coffee at this atmospheric Moorish café overlooking Sidi Bou Saïd's main square.

✉ Place Sidi Bou Saïd 🕐 8am–midnight

Café Sidi Chaabane (£)
Sit outside sipping the house speciality – mint tea sprinkled with pinenuts – while admiring the view of the Gulf of Tunis.

✉ Rue Sidi Chaabane 🕐 Summer 7am–midnight; winter 8–8

TABARKA
Touta (£–££)
Great shady terrace with a view of the port and the fort, and a large choice of fish fresh from the boats coming in.

✉ Porto Corallo ☎ 76 671018 🕐 Lunch, dinner; closed during Ramadan

TUNIS
Café de Paris (£)
Always busy and a convenient meeting place and people-watching spot. One of the few cafés to serve beer.

✉ Corner of avenue Habib Bourguiba and avenue de Carthage 🕐 All day

Capitole Restaurant (££)
Long-established, reasonably priced first-floor restaurant with a particularly good Franco-Tunisian menu.

✉ 60 avenue Habib Bourguiba ☎ 71 256601 🕐 Lunch, dinner

Chez Nous (££)

Photos of famous guests line the walls of this intimate French
restaurant which offers good *à la carte* and set menus.

✉ 5 rue de Marseille ☎ 71 253048 ⏱ Lunch, dinner; closed Sun

Chez Slah (££)

International, Tunisian and French cuisine in an agreeable setting.
The house speciality is seafood fresh from the Gulf of Tunis.
Alcohol and beer served and good selection of wine.

✉ 14 bis rue Pierre de Coubertin ☎ 71 258588 ⏱ Lunch, dinner; closed
Mon

Dar Bel Hadj (££)

Traditional médina restaurant with tables around a lovely courtyard,
and smaller salons on the first floor. Excellent Tunisian cuisine.

✉ 17 rue des Tamis ☎ 71 200894 ⏱ Lunch, dinner; closed Sun

Dar El Jeld (£££)

See page 58.

La Mamma (£)

Pizzas and pasta as well as a range of Tunisian dishes at this
dependable Italian-style restaurant.

✉ 11 rue de Marseille ☎ 71 249106 ⏱ Lunch, dinner

ENTERTAINMENT

Nightlife in the centre of Tunis is limited, apart from **Lounge Bar
Jamaica** on the 10th floor of Hotel el Hana International (avenue
Habib Bourguiba), and **Oscars** (rue de Marseille), with live music at
the weekend. **Le Boeuf sur le Toit,** 3 avenue Fatouma Bourguiba,
in the suburb of La Soukra, is a lively bar-restaurant attracting a
trendy crowd, with a dance floor, good DJs, live music at
weekends and Sunday jazz evenings. The most popular evening
destinations are the cafés in Sidi Bou Said, to drink mint tea,
smoke a *narguileh* (waterpipe) and people-watch. The best night-
club is at **Hotel Plaza Corniche,** rue du Maroc, La Marsa (tel: 71
743489) and at **Villa Didon,** Byrsa Hill, Carthage (tel: 71 733433).

Cap Bon

Standing slightly apart from the rest of the country, the peninsula which ends at Cap Bon is the most productive in Tunisia. With a year-round mild climate, it is known as the Garden of Tunisia; there are citrus and olive groves, and

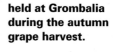

vineyards – although this is a Muslim country there is a long tradition of wine-making, and a wine festival is held at Grombalia during the autumn grape harvest.

On old maps of Tunisia, the town of Nabeul is given as the focal point of the region. It remains the largest town and seat of local government, but for tourists it has been eclipsed by the relentless expansion of near-neighbour Hammamet – the most cosmopolitan resort in Tunisia and a firm favourite with package holidaymakers from all over Europe.

In contrast, on Cap Bon's northern coast there are many small unspoiled villages and long stretches of deserted beach without a hotel in sight.

HAMMAMET

The once pristine coastline of Hammamet attracted wealthy Europeans from the 1920s after Romanian millionaire George Sebastian first built his villa here. Today it is Tunisia's largest resort, pretty much geared up to year-round tourism for every budget.

Easy-going and lively, with a good choice of restaurants, Hammamet's first hotels were built in the centre close to the médina (➤ 114–115) but later developments stretch along the coast almost as far as Nabeul (➤ 118–121), making the most of some of the best beaches in the country.

About 10km (6 miles) from the centre is the resort of Hammamet Yasmine, with a huge marina, trendy hotels and a new médina, all immaculate but somewhat lacking in local flavour.

🞉 E4 ✉ 60km (37 miles) southeast of Tunis 🚌 To Tunis and Nabeul 🚆 Daily train between Tunis and Hammamet

ℹ️ Avenue Habib Bourguiba ☎ 72 262891

Centre International Culturel

Built by George Sebastian in the 1920s, this grand villa was described by architect Frank Lloyd Wright as 'the most beautiful in the world'. Guests have included Winston Churchill and the artist Paul Klee; German field marshall Erwin Rommel used it as his headquarters during World War II. Its open-air theatre is the site of an annual cultural festival in July and August and the building itself is a venue for conferences and art exhibitions.

✉ Avenue des Nations Unies ☎ 72 280410 🕐 Daily 8:30–6 (9–5 in winter) 🖐 Inexpensive ❓ Festival of the Arts: Jul, Aug

Dar Hammamet

A small museum in the médina (➤ 114–115), filled with traditional costumes and a selection of bridal dowries from various parts of the country. The jewellery and embroidery are impressive. There is a fine view of the modern town and the old médina from the rooftop terrace.

✉ The médina ☎ 72 281206 🕐 Daily 9–6 🖐 Moderate

Kasbah

First built in the 15th century, but heavily modified and restored
since, the kasbah is the best place to begin a tour of the médina
(► below). The fort is Hammamet's most conspicuous landmark
and is entered by way of a colossal ramp. There are steep steps up
to the ramparts, from where there are fine views over the white
domes and terraces of the médina and the surrounding coastline.

⊠ Médina ⊕ Daily 8–6 (9–5 in winter) 🍴 Café Sidi Bou Hdid (► 128)

Médina

Much smaller than the médinas of Tunis (► 83), Sousse (► 135)
and Sfax (► 154), but not without its charms, Hammamet's old
town nestles around the kasbah and Grande Mosquée (Great
Mosque). It was built between 1463 and 1474 on the site of a

9th-century settlement. Although the streets closest to the médina walls are lined with souvenir shops, there is a residential area which remains almost completely unspoiled. Wander through the narrow alleys – it's almost impossible to get lost. The studs on the doors are all individually designed and many incorporate the good luck symbols of fish and the hand of Fatima (the daughter of the Prophet Muhammed).

Immediately in front of the médina there is a market, and to the east is an ancient Muslim cemetery.

🍴 Café Sidi Bou Hdid, at the foot of the kasbah (➤ 128)

Pupput

Hammamet's only archaeological site consists of a couple of large Roman villas and a bath house paved with some fine mosaic floors. There are also 4th-century Christian tomb mosaics displayed on a perimeter wall. The ruins are all from the 2nd to the 4th centuries, when Pupput was a prosperous port.

✉ 6km (4 miles) south of the town centre 🕐 Daily 9–7 (to 5 in winter) 🚌 No public transport 👐 Inexpensive

More to see in Cap Bon

EL HAOUARIA

Just outside the village of El Haouaria are the spectacular Ghar el Kebir (Roman Caves; daily 8–7, 9–5 in winter). On the seafront directly opposite the island of Zembra are 24 caves which were quarried for the soft orange limestone used by Carthaginian, Roman and Byzantine builders and sculptors. La Grotte des Chauves-Souris (Cave of the Bats), 4km (2.5 miles) from the town, is home to thousands of bats (now closed). South of the town is Haouaria Plage, an amazing, sheltered stretch of white sands. La Daurade restaurant arranges boat trips around the other caves on the cape, including a barbecue lunch.

F2 ⊠ 14km (8.5 miles) northwest of Kerkouane 🍴 La Daurade (££), next to the caves on the seashore ☎ 72 269080 ❓ Festival of falconry (end May–Jun)

KÉLIBIA

Kélibia is a busy working town with a picturesque fishing port, still unspoiled by tourism and a good base for exploring the Cap Bon region. Overlooking the town is the giant Fort of Kélibia (summer 9–7; winter 9–5), which was built in the 16th century, with excellent views over the harbour, coastline and surrounding countryside. Around the fortress are several excavated Roman remains and mosaics. Kelibia's main beach is not very attractive; a much better beach can be found at Mansoura, 2km (1.2 miles) north of town, although there has been much tourist development there recently.

F2 ⊠ 68km (42 miles) northeast of Hammamet 🍴 Restaurant Anis (£) ⊠ Avenue Erriadh ☎ 72 295777

KERKOUANE

Dating from the 4th century BC, Kerkouane is the world's best example of a purely Punic town. It was destroyed in 236BC and unearthed in 1952; it is now listed as a UNESCO World Heritage Site. Many of the houses had private bathrooms. The little museum has some beautiful jewellery, funerary statues and pottery.

✚ F2 ✉ 9km (5.5 miles) north of Kélibia
☎ 02 294033 ◐ Daily 9–5 (9–4 in winter).
Museum closed Mon ✋ Inexpensive
🚌 Bus from Kélibia or taxi

KORBOUS

A small spa town where people have come to 'take the waters'
since Roman times. There are five springs including the hot and
sulphurous Aïn el Atrous (goat spring), said to be good for skin
complaints and rheumatism. Women regularly slide down the
nearby Zarziha Rock which is believed to cure infertility.

🕂 E3 ✉ 48km (30 miles) east of Tunis 🍴 Restaurant at Résidence des
Thermes (££); Restaurant Dhib on main street (£–££) 🚌 Bus from Tunis

NABEUL

Nabeul used to be known simply as Tunisia's pottery town, but it
has rapidly developed as a resort in its own right, with a clutch of
large beachfront hotels. The main streets are crammed with
pottery shops, souvenir stores and clothing boutiques, and every
Friday the heart of the town is blocked off as Nabeul plays host to
the so-called Camel Market. This huge market attracts busloads of
tourists, and a large part of it is dedicated to crafts and souvenirs.
You are unlikely to come across any real camels, though. For non-
tourist goods the Marché Central (Central Market) is much more
genuine and well worth a visit.

In Roman times Nabeul's major industry was the manufacture of a pungent fish sauce called *garum* which was made by salting the blood and guts of tuna fish and then leaving it in an airtight container for three or four months. During excavations at Roman **Neapolis** on the outskirts of town during the 1960s, several amphorae of the sauce were unearthed – but they appeared to have passed their sell-by date. Neapolis is something of a disappointment if you have visited any of Tunisia's major archaeological sites – there is not much to see apart from a few pillars, some mosaic fragments and a series of pits thought to be the remains of a fish processing factory. The most colourful mosaics, some illustrating episodes from the *Iliad*, are on display in the **Musée**

Régional, as well as finds from around the Cap Bon region. These include sculptures of the Carthaginian moon goddess Tanit, unearthed in 1948 from a temple called Thinissut in the hills above Hammamet; some Carthaginian pieces excavated from Kerkouane (➤ 117); a 2,500-year-old statue of a naked man and a collection of Roman domestic pottery. A new display explains about the Neapolis excavations and the fishing industry.

Nabeul's pottery industry also dates back to Roman times with many of today's designs and popular colours (blue and white, and yellow and green) the same as those used 2,000 years ago. Although pottery can be bought all over Tunisia, Nabeul offers one of the biggest selections. Tourists who hate the idea of haggling can shop for pots and plates at two official tourist shops in the town, where all goods have fixed prices. (Even if you like the idea of haggling it is worth calling in at one of the shops just to get an idea of the true cost of items.) Do not be fooled by one or two other shops in the town displaying signs which suggest they also have set prices. It is just a ploy to entice visitors in – once inside, you will find prices become surprisingly flexible.

Nabeul has a thriving brick and perfume industry; the suburb of Dar Chaabane specializes in stone carving; and the village of Beni Khiar, 2km (1 mile) to the east, is known for its carpet weaving and wool products.

✚ E4 ✉ 65km (40 miles) southeast of Tunis
🚌 Hourly to Tunis; depart from bus station on avenue Habib Thameur ℹ Avenue Taïeb Mehiri ☎ 72 286800

Neapolis

✉ Opposite Hotel Monia Club, just off the route Touristique 🕐 Tue–Sun 9–1, 4–7 (9:30–4 in winter) 💷 Inexpensive

Musée Régional

✉ 44 avenue Bourguiba 🕐 Tue–Sun 9–1, 3–7 (9:30–4 in winter) 💷 Inexpensive

THUBURBO MAJUS

Although it was first settled in the 5th century BC, most of the
ruins at Thuburbo Majus are from later Roman times, when the
town was an important trading centre for the region's agricultural
produce and probably had a population of around 8,000. Like many
of Tunisia's archaeological sites, it is not unusual to have the place
almost completely to yourself. With no guides available, even if
you have a map, it can be quite difficult to make sense of the
sprawling site. The paved open space at the centre is the forum,
which was where political and financial matters were discussed;

the temple, built in AD168, was dedicated to Jupiter, Juno and Minerva; the Winter Baths, with their veined pink marble columns, are up the hill. The Palaestra of the Petronii was a gymnasium (delineated by a line of columns) where young men took part in boxing or wrestling bouts. Many of the best finds from this site, including a statue of Jupiter and some fine mosaics, are now kept in the Musée du Bardo in Tunis (➤ 48–49).

➕ C4 ✉ 65km (40 miles) west of Hammamet ⏰ Daily 8–7 (8.30–5.30 in winter) 🚌 Buses between Tunis and Kairouan drop off at the turn-off, then a 15-min walk ♿ Inexpensive 🍴 Small café at entrance (£)

ZAGHOUAN

Zaghouan is a sleepy, unspoiled agricultural town between Hammamet and Thuburbo Majus, with cobbled streets and tiled roofs. Water from Mount Zaghouan was used to supply Carthage by way of a 70km (43-mile) Roman aqueduct, parts of which can still be seen along the Tunis–Zaghouan road. The Temple des Eaux (Temple of the Waters), built by the Emperor Hadrian in AD130, is the town's greatest sight.

➕ D4 ✉ 30km (18.5 miles) west of Hammamet 🍴 Café at Temple des Eaux (£); La Source on main street (£–££) 🚌 Frequent buses from Tunis, Nabeul and Hammamet

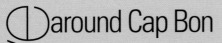

around Cap Bon

A chance to get out of the busy resorts to see some Punic ruins and wonderful beaches.

Head out of Hammamet on the road to Nabeul (▶ 118–121), about 10km (6 miles) north.

Stroll through Nabeul checking out the pottery worksho

Continue on the coastal road north.

After 12km (7.5 miles), the next town, Korba, is a big agricultural centre with a lively Sunday souq. The salt marshes attract migrant birds in spring and autumn.

Pass through Menzel Temime to Kélibia (▶ 116).

Visit the 16th-century fortress and have a drink at the Café du Fort at the entrance, with superb views of the Mediterranean and the unspoiled fishing port. North of Kélibia is Mansoura where, a further 2km (1.2 miles) north, is a superb beach with small coves.

Halfway between Kélibia and El Haouaria follow the signpost to Kerkouane, 2km (1.2 miles) off the road.

Visit the charming and idyllic remains of the Punic city of Kerkouane (▶ 117).

Continue on to the beautiful town of El Haouaria.

The town has several caves: Ghar El Kebir and the Bat Caves (▶ 116). Stop for lunch or continue to one of Cap Bon's beautiful beaches, Haouaria Plage.

Return to Hammamet on the same road, or continue back down along the west coast of Cap Bon, heading back for Hammamet via Menzel Bouzelfa, Beni Khalled and the vineyards of Grombalia.

Distance 140km (87 miles)
Time All day, including swims, visits and lunch stops
Start/end point Hammamet ✚ E4
Lunch Picnic on the beach or La Daurade at El Haouaria

HOTELS

HAMMAMET

Belle Vue (£)

The advantage of this hotel is its superb beachfront location close to the médina, but the rooms do look a bit dilapidated.

✉ Avenue Assad ibn el Fourat ☎ 72 281121

Dar Hayet (££–£££)

See page 74.

Hasdrubal Thalassa & Spa (£££)

The most luxurious resort hotel in town, the Hasdrubal offers sumptuous accommodation, an amazing spa and all watersports facilities on a superb stretch of beach.

✉ Zone Touristique Yasmine ☎ 72 244000; www.hasdrubal-hotel.com

Miramar (£££)

The hotel is well maintained and sits on a pleasantly uncrowded strip of beach. Shops and restaurants just across the road.

✉ Rue de Nevers (4km/2.5 miles from the centre) ☎ 72 280344

Les Orangers (£££)

This all-inclusive beach resort is some way out of the town centre. It offers a sandy beach, colourful gardens, a health club and a full programme of entertainment day and night. Perfect for families.

✉ Rue de Nevers ☎ 72 280144; www.tunisia-orangers.com

Résidence Hammamet (£–££)

One of Hammamet's best tourist hotels. All rooms sleep up to four and have mini-kitchens. There is a rooftop terrace with a swimming pool and a private beach. Very close to the médina.

✉ Avenue Habib Bourguiba ☎ 72 280733; www.hammamet-residence.com

Residence Romane (££)

This family-run hotel is not a large package hotel. Rooms are attractively decorated, with en-suite bathrooms and balconies.

✉ Rue Assad ben Fourat, 15-min walk from centre ☎ 72 263103

Riu Palace Ocean (££)

Popular large resort hotel, set in vast gardens, with excellent service, sports facilities and modern, comfortable rooms with large bathrooms.

✉ Barraket Essahel, 8km (5 miles) from centre ☎ 72 227227; www.riu.com

Shératon (£££)

An extensive resort hotel with rooms built in small clusters in lush gardens. Six tennis courts, swimming pool and children's play area.

✉ Route Touristique Hammamet Sud (6km/4 miles from town centre)
☎ 72 226555; www.sheraton.com

EL HAOUARIA
L'Épervier (££)

Off the main street and built round a pretty courtyard. A clean and comfortable hotel with almost the only restaurant in town.

✉ 3 avenue Habib Bourguiba ☎ 72 297017

KELIBIA
Palmarina (££)

Newish hotel with swimming pool, café/bar and restaurant. The sun terrace overlooks a small beach and the fishing harbour.

✉ Avenue des Martyrs ☎ 72 274062

NABEUL
Hôtel Vime Lido (£££)

Large complex with cottages in the grounds as well as a main hotel building. Every facility you would expect from a popular package destination.

✉ Avenue 7 Novembre ☎ 72 362988; www.vimehoteles.com

Les Jasmins (££)

In a secluded tree-lined road five minutes' walk from a quiet beach. Rooms are in two-storey blocks set in gardens. There's a swimming pool and seafood restaurant also on site.

✉ Rue Abou el Kacem Chabbi (just outside Nabeul town centre)
☎ 72 285343; www.hotellesjasmins.com

Pension Les Oliviers (£–££)

A cut above the average guest house with clean rooms and en
suite bathrooms in a large modern house. Close to the beach and
a minute's walk from the Hôtel Les Jasmins (➤ 127).

✉ Rue Abou el-Kacem Chabbi ☎ 72 286865

RESTAURANTS

EL HAOUARIA
L'Épervier (£–££)

Straightforward food at this popular venue busy with tour groups
at lunchtime and a local crowd in the evening.

✉ 3 avenue Habib Bourguiba ☎ 72 297017 🕓 Lunch, dinner

HAMMAMET
Café Sidi Bou Hdid (£)

Also known as Café des Muriers. An atmospheric domed café
which is at its best on warm summer evenings, when customers
spill out on to the surrounding ramparts. *The* place for mint tea.

✉ Seafront end of the médina 🕓 All day

Chez Achour (££)

See page 58.

Dar Lella (££)

One of the few places serving more good upmarket Tunisian
cuisine, in pleasant surroundings, both in the Berber-style dining
room and the garden.

✉ Just off avenue du Kuwayt ☎ 72 280140 🕓 Lunch, dinner

Le Corsaire (££–£££)

Upmarket seafood restaurant in a boat. The fish and seafood
specialities are excellent, and the top deck is a great place to
watch the world go by.

✉ Port Yasmine ☎ 72 240323 🕓 Lunch, dinner

La Pergola (££)

Pleasant location with a large outside terrace awash with greenery. Everything from soups and salads to grilled meats and fish.

✉ Avenue Habib Bourguiba ☎ 72 280993 🕐 Lunch, dinner

Restaurant Barberousse (££)

Hugely popular in the summer months with its roof terrace overlooking the médina. Both view and food are good value.

✉ Entrance to the médina ☎ 72 280037 🕐 Lunch, dinner

Restaurant La Brise (£)

Salads, grills and couscous served in a simple but colourful modern interior. A good place for lunch.

✉ 2 avenue de la République ☎ 72 280073 🕐 Lunch, dinner

La Scala (£££)

The pasta is excellent at this intimate Italian restaurant.

✉ Off avenue des Nations Unies ☎ 72 280768 🕐 Lunch, dinner; closed in winter. Reservation advisable

Les Trois Moutons (££–£££)

One of the best restaurants in town, with excellent meat and fish dishes. Offers an extensive menu and a good value set dinner.

✉ Centre Commercial, avenue Habib Bourguiba ☎ 72 280981 🕐 Lunch, dinner

KÉLIBIA

Anis (£)

Very good value restaurant in the town centre offering Tunisian specialities and pleasant service.

✉ Avenue Erriadh ☎ 72 295777 🕐 Lunch, dinner

Restaurant El-Mansourah (££)

Choose grilled fish and salad with a bottle of the local Muscat de Kélibia, a refreshing medium-dry white wine.

✉ Out beyond Kélibia's fort, southern end of Mansoura Beach ☎ 72 295167 🕐 Lunch, dinner

NABEUL
Café Errachida (£)
A welcoming café specializing in mint tea served with tempting sticky cakes.

✉ Avenue Habib Thameur (at the junction with avenue Habib Bourguiba)

🕐 All day

Restaurant Bon Kif (££–£££)
Stylish Tunisian restaurant where tourists and locals gather for long, lazy seafood lunches.

✉ Avenue Marbella ☎ 72 222783 🕐 Lunch, dinner

Restaurant de l'Olivier (£££)
This restaurant is not cheap, but it offers gourmet French cooking in smart surroundings. The wine list includes imported wines as well as some that have been produced locally.

✉ 6 avenue Hedi Chaker ☎ 72 286613 🕐 Lunch, dinner

Restaurant Slovenia (£–££)
See page 59.

ENTERTAINMENT

NIGHTCLUBS
Buena Vista Social Club
✉ Avenue de la Paix, next to Hotel Serail, Hammamet Sud

Calypso
✉ Avenue Moncef Bey, Hammamet ☎ 72 227530

Cotton Club
✉ Avenue Moncef Bey, Hammamet ☎ 72 227053

Manhattan
✉ Hammamet Sud, Hammamet ☎ 72 226226

Le Pacha
✉ Avenue Moncef Bey, Hammamet ☎ 72 226462

Central Tunisia

The coast of central Tunisia is a booming holiday region, with the growing beach resorts of Sousse and Monastir. Sfax and Sousse are a delight with their ancient city walls, vibrant souqs, fascinating museums and thriving fishing ports. Mahdia, in comparison, is a delightful, sleepy backwater with a gorgeous unspoiled médina and smaller hotels. Kairouan, Tunisia's most holy city, combines its spiritual role as a national centre for prayer and pilgrimage with the secular demands of its commercial carpet-making industry.

Sfax

The surrounding richly fertile plain, known as the Sahel, stretches down the central east coast, embracing the resorts of Mahdia and Monastir. Its vast numbers of olive trees have been the mainstay of the region's economy since Roman times. In contrast, the western Tell, once forested, is now a hauntingly desolate terrain only suitable for rough grazing. Its main attraction is the isolated Roman ruin of Sbeïtla.

SOUSSE

Sousse used to be just an excursion destination for day trippers; now it is a busy holiday centre in its own right. Packed with atmosphere and hundreds of years of history, Tunisia's leading city beach resort offers a good selection of quality hotels, a wide choice of affordable restaurants and endless possibilities for shopping.

Along with Carthage (➤ 86–91) and Utique (➤ 103), Sousse was one of the Phoenicians' three great coastal cities, with the earliest archaeological finds dating from the 6th century BC. In the 7th century AD the city fell to Arab invaders who left it in ruins, but in AD 790 the foundations for a new city were laid, and many remnants of this time still survive today.

✚ R18 ✉ 143km (89 miles) from Tunis 🍴 Plenty of choice (£–£££)
🚊 On the Tunis–Gabès line 🚍 To Monastir and Mahdia 🚌 Buses to south and north ✈ International airport at Skanès–Monastir, 15km (9 miles) away
ℹ 1 avenue Habib Bourguiba ☎ 73 225157 🕐 Mon–Sat 8:30–1, 3–5:45

Catacombs of the Good Shepherd

The catacombs could be developed into a major tourist attraction, but for the moment their appeal is limited. There are claimed to be more than 15,000 marble tombs from the 2nd to the 5th centuries spread throughout a 5.5km (3.5-mile) network of tunnels, but currently only one very small section is open to the public.

✉ About 1km (half a mile) west of the médina, off rue Abdou Hamed el Ghazali 🕐 Tue–Sun 9–12, 3–7 (9–12, 2–6 in winter) ✋ Inexpensive

Grande Bain Maure Sidi Bouraoui

The Sidi Bouraoui Baths is one of the best places to try a traditional hammam or *bain maure* (Turkish bath) with lengthy separate sessions for men and women. The masseur (or for women, a masseuse) uses a coarse glove known as a *tfal* which leaves the skin pink and tingling. Expect to spend at least two hours here to make the most of the experience.

✉ 23 rue el Aghlaba (behind Mosquée Abd el Kader). 🕐 5am–1pm for men;
1:30–7:30pm for women 🖐 Moderate

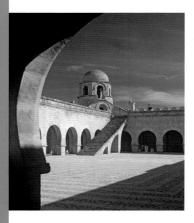

Grande Mosquée

Respectful dress is required for a visit to the Great Mosque, which looks like a fortress, with turrets and crenellations. Originally built in 851 by a freed slave called Mudam on the orders of the Aghlabite ruler Abdul Abbas, the internal courtyard has the pleasantly uncomplicated architecture common to many Islamic places of worship, the only decoration being a single line of Koranic inscription. A wide stairway leads to the walls; the minaret and prayer hall are not open to non-Muslims.

✉ Rue el Aghlaba ⏰ Sat–Thu 8–2, Fri 8–1 💷 Inexpensive

Kasbah Sousse Museum

Situated in the southwest corner of the médina (➤ opposite) the Kasbah Sousse Museum not only offers a superb panoramic view across the city, but has a fine and most interesting collection of mosaics rivalling those at the Musée du Bardo (➤ 48–49). Most of the mosaics date from the 3rd and 4th centuries, with the depiction of the Triumph of Bacchus among the most noted. The adjoining courtyard is a pleasant place to sit among the palm trees, flowers and bits of marble column and stone tablets.

 Off boulevard Marechal Tito  Summer Tue–Thu 9–12, 3–7, Fri–Sun 9–6; winter Tue–Thu 9–12, 3–6, Fri–Sun 9–6. Closed public hols

Inexpensive

Médina

The médina is the old heart of an area of the city with great appeal. It is still surrounded by the 9th-century walls. The *ribat* (► 137) and Grande Mosquée (► opposite) are at the main entrance to the médina, and on the opposite side is the kasbah with the kasbah museum (► opposite). Following the wall westward from the *ribat* is Dar Es Sid (summer daily 10–7, winter 10–6), a beautifully restored traditional home which is now a museum illustrating life in the médina. The main shopping street in the souqs, rue de Paris, has mainly shops selling cheap tourist souvenirs. The rue de la Kasbah, leading right off the rue de France to the kasbah, has shops selling more authentic crafts and local produce.

Many cafés (£)

Musée de Kalaout el Koubba

The Museum of Kalaout el Koubba is in one of the most unusual buildings in the médina (➤ 135), with a striking zigzag decoration on the dome. Dating from around the 11th century and believed to have been either an audience chamber for a neighbouring Fatimid palace or one of the hot rooms of a hammam, it has had many uses over the years, most recently as an art gallery and café. Today the museum's displays focus on the traditional life of the médina with ceramics, kitchen equipment, musical instruments and national costumes.

✉ Rue Souq el Reba 🕐 Mon–Thu, Sat 9:30–1, 3–5:30, Sun 10–2
✋ Inexpensive

Ribat

The *ribat* (fortified monastery) was built early in the 9th century as one of a chain of fortresses stretching along the Mediterranean coast to defend North Africa from European invaders. It was completed by the Aghlabids in 821, incorporating an earlier structure built in 790 which itself was sited on the ruins of a 6th-century Byzantine fortress. The large central courtyard which slopes downwards to a cistern is surrounded by a series of small cells which were used by the warrior-monks as tiny study-bedrooms.

A room above the main gate has four slits in the floor through which boiling olive oil was poured on unwelcome visitors. For many visitors, though, the most interesting part of the *ribat* is the view from the ramparts over the médina (➤ 135). There is often a queue to climb the 75 steps to the top of the circular tower for views of the town.

✉ Rue el Aghlaba 🕐 Daily 8–7 (8–5:30 in winter) ✋ Inexpensive

a drive from Sousse to El Jem

This scenic drive includes the tourist town of Monastir (➤ 140–143) and is ideal for a day trip from Sousse (or Port El Kantaoui, ➤ 150–151). Starting soon after breakfast is recommended.

Head southwest out of Sousse past the louages *station following signs to Sfax and Kairouan. Drive through the suburbs of Zaouiet Sousse and Messadine. Soon after leaving M'Saken join the 1 and head south on a long, straight road flanked by row upon row of olive trees.*

It takes just over an hour to get to El Jem (➤ 38–39) driving at a leisurely pace. It is impossible to miss the amphitheatre which dominates the small town and can

be seen clearly from the approach road. Finding somewhere to park may be more difficult. Allow at least 90 minutes for the amphitheatre and the Archaeological Museum.

From the museum turn left on avenue Taïeb Mehiri and continue along avenue Belhaouane, taking the 87 to Mahdia. Drive for 10km (6 miles) passing through the village of Telelsa and then turn left at the signpost for Moknine. Reaching a cross-roads after about 12km (7.5 miles) head straight on into the village of El Fhoul, reaching Moknine (famous for its pottery) 16km (10 miles) later. Follow signs to Monastir 30km (18.5 miles) further north.

The *ribat* and Bourguiba Mausoleum are among Monastir's main tourist attractions (➤ 140–143). The town is also good for souvenir shopping.

Head out of town following signposts for Tunis. Take the A1 north for the easy 20km (12.5-mile) drive back to Sousse.

Distance 160km (100 miles)
Time Seven hours including stops
Start/end point Sousse ✚ R18
Lunch At Hotel Julius (£) next to train station in El Jem

MONASTIR

Until the 1960s Monastir was a fairly typical Tunisian town, but since then it has been transformed into a huge tourist resort. The development has more or less swallowed the old town and its original character, but what is left is worth visiting. It has an attractive 400-berth marina and an old fishing port. Most of the tourist hotels are 6km (4 miles) west of the town centre in the suburb of Skanès, near the international airport.

➕ R18 ✉ 160km (100 miles) south of Tunis 🚌 From Sousse 🚃 Frequent departures to Tunis and Sousse ❓ Monastir International Festival in summer ℹ Rue de l'Indépendance 🕓 Mon–Sat 8–6. Tourist office also at Monastir Airport ☎ 73 461205 🕓 24 hours

Bourguiba Mausolée

In the early years of his presidency, Habib Bourguiba built himself an elaborate mausoleum in the centre of the Monastir, where he was born. Its twin minarets and golden dome make it instantly recognizable. At its foot is a kiosk commemorating those who died fighting for Tunisia's independence. A statue of Bourguiba as a schoolboy stands in the place du Gouvernorat.

✉ Top end of Sidi el Mazeri Cemetery 🕓 Mon–Thu 2–4:30, Fri–Sun 9–4:30 (until 6pm in summer) ✋ Free, but dress modestly

Médina

A great chunk of Monastir's médina was demolished in the 1960s in the course of a misguided modernization plan and with it the Old Town district lost much of its heart. Dedicated to protecting the médina from any further development (a somewhat lost cause) is the **Association de Sauvegarde de Médina** (City Safe-Keeping Association). Its centre, built around a whitewashed courtyard shaded by an orange tree, provides a welcome oasis from the surrounding bustle.

Association de Sauvegarde de Médina

✉ Rue du 2 Mars 🕓 Tue–Sun 9–1, 3–7 (9–12, 2–6 in winter)

Musée du Costume Traditionnel

The stone-floored, somewhat spartan Museum of Traditional
Costume contains an attractively presented collection of
impressive outfits worn by couples on their wedding day and
for many days following the ceremony. In the 18th and 19th
centuries it was traditional for the bride's dress to be made by
her mother and sisters, which sometimes took several years
because of the huge amount of intricate embroidery involved.
The men's costumes are much simpler.

✉ Avenue de l'Indépendance 🕐 Tue–Mon 9–1, 4–7 (9–4 in winter)
✋ Inexpensive

Ribat

Founded in AD796, the *ribat* has been reworked and restored so
many times that there is little left of the original structure. One
surviving section from earliest times is the prayer hall, which
is now used as a Museum of Islamic Arts. Exhibits include

fragments of 12th-century weaving, Egyptian fabrics, samples of Islamic writings and gold jewellery from Persia. The Nador tower offers spectacular views over the town centre and corniche.

The *ribat* has provided the backdrop for scenes in several major films including *Jesus of Nazareth* and *The Life of Brian*. Connected

to the southern gate is the Grande Mosquée (Great Mosque), built at the same time as the *ribat* and médina walls. It is closed to non-Muslims.

✉ Behind the route de la Corniche ☎ 73 461272
🕐 8–7 (8:30–5:30 in winter)
✋ Inexpensive (includes entry to the Museum of Islamic Arts)

More to See in Central Tunisia

EL JEM
Best places to see, ➤ 38–39.

EL KEF
El Kef – which means 'rock' in Arabic – refers to the town's
dramatic setting on a rocky outcrop just below the summit of Jebel
Dyr. Considered to be the capital of the Tell region, which covers
much of Central Tunisia, El Kef is Tunisia's most significant inland
centre after Kairouan. It was a fortress town from 450BC, and tools
have been found in surrounding caves and woodland dating back
50,000 years. In Roman times El Kef became an important trading
post. Aïn el Kef is a spring which may well have been the reason
for a town being built here; it has been venerated for centuries and
a small shrine still attracts votive offerings.

El Kef is a pleasant town with a picturesque médina, where
Jews, Christians and Muslims have lived together for centuries.
Start a visit at the tranquil place Sidi Bou Makhlouf at the foot of
the kasbah, with the elegant 17th-century Mosquée de Sidi Bou
Makhlouf and the 4th-century basilica converted into the Jamaa
el Kebir (Great Mosque) in the 8th century, the town's oldest

mosque, now
closed to the
public. El Kef's
kasbah consists
of two parts. The
older, larger fort
was first built in
Byzantine times,
later remodelled
by the Turks; the
other was built in
the early 19th

century. The nearby **Musée Regional des Arts et Traditions Populaires** (Regional Museum of Popular Arts and Traditions) focuses on the culture of the Berber people, with displays of clothes, jewellery and household objects.

✚ K8 ✉ 170km (105 miles) southwest of Tunis 🚌 To Tunis from the Gare Routiere SNT 🍴 Hotel-Restaurant Vénus (➤ 157)

🛈 The Artisanat Dar El Medina (The Association for the Protection of the Medina) acts as an informal tourist office ✉ Place de l'Independence

Kasbah
🕐 Daily 7–7 ✋ Free

Musée Regional des Arts et Traditions Populaires
✉ Place Ben Aissa ☎ 78 221503 🕐 9–1, 4:30–7 (9:30–4 in winter) ✋ Inexpensive

ÎLES KERKENNAH
Best places to see, ➤ 40–41.

KAIROUAN
Best places to see, ➤ 44–45.

MAHDIA

Set on a peninsula, Mahdia still clings to its old way of life as much as it can, with its weaving industry and thriving fishing port. Its small médina is the most obvious sign of the town's changing fortunes. Nearly every shop and stall is now geared towards tourists since the creation of a burgeoning *zone touristique* 6km (4 miles) west of the town centre, where the best beaches are to be found.

Mahdia's history dates from the 10th century when it was the capital of the Fatimid dynasty. All that remains of the town's fortifications is the Skifa el-Kahla (Dark Gate), which stands at the entrance to the médina. Next to it is the **Archaeological Museum,** with exhibits from Punic, Roman and Fatimid times and a collection of traditional costumes.

Take a walk along the main thoroughfare, rue Obaidallah el Mehdi. At the end of the street there is the picture-perfect place du Caire, where cafés, some with seats shaded by trees and

vines, serve refreshments. Just beyond the square is the Grande Mosquée (Great Mosque), built in the 1960s. The large fortress which stands on the highest point of the peninsula is the **Borj el Kebir,** a 16th-century Turkish fort which offers excellent views over the town, port and surrounding Muslim cemetery. Just behind the Borj el Kebir, on rue Mohammed Abd Essalam, is Dar Sghir (winter daily 9–6, until 11pm in summer), a typical Mahdian house, now opened to the public as a museum illustrating the traditional life of a Mahdian family. The port may look familiar: it was used as the setting for the German invasion of Benghazi in the Oscar-winning film *The English Patient*, starring Ralph Fiennes.

➕ S19 ✉ 62km (38.5 miles) from Sousse
🍴 Cafés in place du Caire (£) 🚆 One train daily to and from Tunis from the station on avenue Farhat Hached, plus regular metro services to Monastir and Sousse 🚌 Almost hourly buses to Sousse and Sfax
ℹ Rue el Moez (just inside the médina by the Skifa el Kahla) ☎ 73 681098

Archaeological Museum
➕ Place de l'Indépendance 🕐 9–1, 4–7 (9–4 in winter). Closed Mon ✋ Inexpensive

Borj el Kebir
➕ Rue du Borj 🕐 Tue–Sun 9–1, 4–7 (9–4 in winter) ✋ Inexpensive

a walk around Mahdia

This walk can be done at any time of the day, but is best in the early morning or late afternoon.

Start at the fishing harbour, which is still the focal point of Mahdia despite the onslaught of tourism.

Wander around the harbour watching the fishermen unload their catch or repair their nets; call in at the daily fish market, where traders auction fish straight from the sea.

Turn right out of the harbour entrance on to the seafront path (rue du Borj), which leads to the Grande Mosquée (Great Mosque) and Borj el Kebir (▶ 147). Between the two is a fenced-off excavation site. With the fort on your left, branch off to walk through the cemetery with its simple white gravestones. Follow the path round to the

tiny red lighthouse, passing the gardens and rocks to the right which form Cap d'Afrique. Turning the corner of the windswept headland, notice the whitewashed roofs of the zone touristique *in the distance. Walk back towards Mahdia town along avenue 7 Novembre, with its traditional seafront houses.*

On this street you will pass the Association de Sauvegarde de Médina on the left, in a grand old house, which offers information about the médina and renovation projects.

Turn left up the alleyway running alongside the Hotel Al-Jazira, checking out the weaving workshops on the way. Follow it around to emerge next to the tourist information centre and the main entrance to the médina. Stroll down rue Obaidallah el Mehdi to the shaded place du Caire and then turn right by the side of Mosquée Mustapha Hamza, which leads to a cluster of shops and cafés on rue des Fatmides.

Distance 4km (2.5 miles)
Time Two hours including stops
Start point Fishing port
End point Rue des Fatmides
Lunch Restaurant de la Medina (£), in same building as fish market

PORT EL KANTAOUI

Purpose-built around a picturesque marina which now draws luxury yachts from all over the world, Port El Kantaoui opened in 1979 and has been Tunisia's most outstandingly successful tourist centre. With the look and feel of an elite residential district, it is the sort of development where you would expect to find the homes of top politicians, diplomats or the fabulously wealthy. The only difference is that the residents of this smart enclave are mainly package holidaymakers, often first-time visitors looking for a gentle introduction to Tunisia. Although it's equally popular with families and older couples, who like its reassuringly familiar ambience and strong sense of safety, detractors criticize Port El Kantaoui for its artificiality. It's also not unusual to find holidaymakers outnumbering Tunisians ten to one.

Millions of dinars have been poured into landscaping, with palm trees, shrubs and grass borders lining every road and not a tatty bit of paintwork in sight. The resort's hotels are equally sparkling; white-washed palaces with terraced gardens awash with bougainvillaea.

The first-built hotels have the advantage of being closest to the marina and are also generally thought to offer the best quality. Some of the newest accommodation can involve a good ten-minute walk to the shops and restaurants surrounding the harbour. Port El Kantaoui is practically self-sufficient and apart from the obligatory souvenir shops it has banks, a supermarket, hairdressers and a newsagent.

Sailing trips in glass-bottomed cruisers, fishing boats or in an imitation pirate's galleon are available from the marina. There is also a diving club and nearby riding stables have horses and camels for hire. Port El Kantaoui's pride and joy is its beautifully manicured 36-hole championship golf course. There are no membership requirements and while golfers with their own equipment are welcome, those who prefer to travel light can rent everything from clubs to caddies at very reasonable rates. Most hotels will arrange bookings and pre-set tee-times with the club.

✚ R18 ✉ 134km (83 miles) south of Tunis 🍴 Large choice of restaurants Buses to Sousse operate along the main road just outside the entrance to Port El Kantaoui ❶ The marina ⏰ Mon–Sat 7:30–7 (8–6 in winter)

SBEÏTLA

Sbeïtla is the most southerly of Tunisia's major Roman sites. Established at the beginning of the first century on the site of an early Numidian settlement, it was known as Sufetula and reached the height of its prosperity towards the end of the 2nd century. The town has realized the attraction of the Roman site nearby, and the local government is trying hard to develop more of an infrastructure to receive visitors. There is a massive triumphal arch just before the entrance to the archaeological site and a museum; other interesting ruins include the forum built in AD139, the well-preserved baths with their under-floor heating system and a more modern structure, the 6th-century Basilica of St Vitalis, with a beautiful baptismal font covered in mosaics.

✚ L10 ✉ 117km (73 miles) west of Kairouan ⏰ 7–7 (8:30–5:30 in winter) 🚌 Daily buses to Kairouan from car park off rue Habib Thameur ✋ Moderate

SFAX

Tunisia's second city is rarely visited by holidaymakers except perhaps those with a couple of hours to spare while awaiting ferries to Îles Kerkennah (▶ 40–41). Although it is mainly an industrial city with factories sprawling along the coastline, the city centre is attractively compact and very underrated. One of the joys of Sfax is being able to wander through its streets and souqs without hassle from over-eager traders.

Founded in AD849 near the site of a small Roman town, Taparura, Sfax quickly became prosperous by trading in the products of the Sahel's olive trees. Remaining largely independent until the beginning of the 17th century, it strongly resisted the imposition of the French Protectorate in 1881. In response, French marines stormed the city, defacing its mosques and killing several hundred people. Hedi Chaker and Farhat Hached, two of the Tunisia's trade union leaders involved in securing the country's independence and whose names are seen on street signs across the country, both hailed from Sfax.

➕ R22 ✉ 270km (168 miles) southeast of Tunis 🚆 Five services a day (four in winter) to El Jem, Sousse and Tunis from the station at the eastern end of avenue Habib Bourguiba 🚌 To Tunis and Sousse ⛴ Regular daytime services to Îles Kerkennah ✈ Two Tuninter flights a week to Tunis

ℹ Avenue Mohammed Hedi Khefecha ☎ 74 211040 🕐 Mon–Thu 9–1, 3–5:30, Fri–Sat 9–1

Archaeological Museum

The archaeological collection is housed in the Town Hall, a grand colonial building with a dome and clock tower. Although it only has six exhibition rooms there are several items of interest, including an unusual 3rd-century Roman mosaic of children wrestling, Christian funerary mosaics and Roman and Muslim tombs. There are also displays of Roman wall paintings, glass and prehistoric tools from Gafsa (➤ 170).

✉ Junction of avenues Habib Bourguiba and Hedi Chaker ☎ 74 229744 🕐 Mon–Sat, 8:30–1, 3–6 (8:30–3 in summer) ✋ Inexpensive

Médina

The old town in Sfax has one of the best-preserved and most atmospheric médinas in the country. Surrounded by massive stone walls originally built by the Aghlabites in the 9th century, it is a hive of activity with dozens of first-floor workshops for tailors, engravers and furniture-makers. At the heart of a labyrinth of narrow streets and *impasses* is the Grande Mosquée (Great Mosque), which was started in AD849 and extensively rebuilt in the 10th century. It is closed to non-Muslims. The best view of its celebrated, several-tiered minaret is from place Souk el Djemaa.

Sfax's covered souqs run between the Grande Mosquée and rue des Forgerons. Immediately beyond Bab Jebli, the oldest surviving gateway to the médina, is a large food market. Go early in the day as the night's fishing catch is unloaded from cold storage vans. An even bigger daily fish market operates opposite the docks on avenue Ali Bach Hamba.

✉ Main entrance on avenue Ali Belhouane 🍴 Many cafés (£) 🎟 Free

Musée Régional des Arts et Traditions

The Regional Museum of Arts and Traditions (also known as the Dar Jellouli Museum), is at the heart of the médina in a handsome 17th-century town house, the former home of one of Tunisia's most influential families, and gives an idea of what life would have been like for an upper class family in Sfax in the 19th century. The house itself is just as interesting as the exhibits, with its white paved floors, tiled walls and carved wood ceilings. As well as displays of furniture, traditional costumes and jewellery, there are special sections on calligraphy and painting on glass.

✉ Rue de le Driba ☎ 74 211186 🕐 Tue–Sun 9:30–4:30 🎟 Inexpensive

HOTELS

ÎLES KERKENNAH
Grand (££)

Secluded beachfront hotel with spacious rooms, a swimming pool and tennis courts. Cycling and horse-riding available nearby.

✉ Sidi Frej ☎ 74 489861; www.grand-hotel-kerkennah.com.tn

KAIROUAN
La Kasbah (£££)

The elegant rooms are spacious and set around a large courtyard with a heated swimming pool. The hotel has two restaurants and a pleasant *café maure* in the old stables

✉ Avenue Ibn el Jazzar, northern end of the médina ☎ 77 237301; www.goldenyasmin.com

MAHDIA
Hotel Médina (£)

Charming budget option in a large médina house with simple but clean and very cheerful rooms around a courtyard.

✉ Rue el Kaem ☎ 73 694664

Le Phénix (££)

This pleasant, contemporary boutique hotel, whose rooms have floor-to-ceiling windows and large balconies, is the only upmarket accommodation outside the large beach resorts in the *zone touristique*. The service is efficient, with an excellent Tunisian restaurant and a bar, and it's only a short walk from the beach and the médina.

✉ Avenue Habib Bourguiba ☎ 73 690101

MONASTIR
Yasmine (£–££)

Charming, family-run pension with single and double rooms and a licensed restaurant.

✉ Route de la Falaise ☎ 73 501546

SFAX

Les Oliviers (££–£££)

Stunning hotel on the main square, in a Moorish-colonial style. The rooms are elegant, with mahogany wood and a contemporary touch. Very pleasant café in the atrium for a coffee or light lunch.

✉ Avenue Hedi Chaker ☎ 74 201999; www.goldenyasmin.com

Thyna (£–££)

The Thyna offers modern, immaculately clean and comfortable rooms overlooking an elegant square with café terraces.

✉ 37 rue Habib Maazoun ☎ 74 225317

SOUSSE

Abou Nawas Boujafaar (£££)

Plush beachfront hotel which is equally well placed for shopping and eating out. Facilities include a couple of popular bars, a terrace restaurant and a thalassotherapy spa.

✉ Avenue Habib Bourguiba ☎ 73 226030; www.abounawas.com.tn

Claridge (£)

See page 74.

El Hana Beach (£££)

A popular family hotel in colourful gardens. Guests can use the facilities of the neighbouring El Hana and Chems El Hana hotels.

✉ Boulevard de la Corniche ☎ 73 226900

Médina (£)

One of the best hotels in the médina. Rooms have en-suite bathrooms and open on to a small courtyard.

✉ 15 rue Othman Osman ☎ 73 221722

Paris (£)

Beautifully maintained budget hotel just inside the walls of the médina. Friendly management, lots of atmosphere – but shared washing facilities.

✉ 15 rue Rempart Nord ☎ 73 220564

Sousse Azur (££)

Friendly, comfortable, close to the beach and good value for money.

✉ 5 rue Amilcar ☎ 73 227760

RESTAURANTS

EL KEF
Vénus (££)

One of the best restaurants in town, offering good-value set-price meals and an extensive à la carte choice. Serves alcohol.

✉ Rue Farhat Hached ☎ 78 204695 🕔 Lunch, dinner; closed Fri night

ÎLES KERKENNAH
La Sirène (££)

Excellent fresh fish in a venue overlooking the sea.

✉ Remla beachfront ☎ 74 281118 🕔 Lunch, dinner

MAHDIA
Le Neptune (££)

See page 59.

Restaurant el-Moez (£)

Popular with local people; fish soup and *kammounia* (meat stew) are among the specialities served here.

✉ In a small side street between Skifa el Kahla and rue des Fatmides
🕔 Lunch, dinner

MONASTIR
Dar Chakra (£–££)

See page 58.

La Plage (££)

Dine overlooking the sea at this restauarant close to the fishing port; fresh fish is the speciality of the house.

✉ Place du 3 Août ☎ 73 461124 🕔 Lunch, dinner; closed Fri

PORT EL KANTAOUI
La Daurade (££–£££)
See page 59.

SFAX
Chez Nous (££)
The food here is good, and the service friendly. Tunisian specialities include various *ojjas* (egg dishes) and fish couscous.
✉ 26 rue Patrice Lumumba ☎ 74 227128 🕓 Lunch, dinner

Le Corail (£££)
Elegant, rather formal restaurant popular with wealthy Sfaxian families, serving excellent fish and seafood dishes.
✉ 39 rue Habib Mazoun ☎ 74 227301 🕓 Lunch, dinner

SOUSSE
Le Lido (££)
See page 59.

Tip Top (££)
Aimed at the holiday market, but also attracting Tunisians. A popular choice, offering a warm welcome, cosy ambience in a restored Turkish house and excellent choice of food.
✉ Boulevard de la Corniche ☎ 73 226158 🕓 Lunch, dinner

ENTERTAINMENT

CASINO
Casino Club Caraïbe
✉ Boulevard 7 Novembre, Sousse ☎ 73 211777

NIGHTCLUBS
Bora Bora
✉ Boulevard du 7 Novembre, Sousse; www.boraboratunisia.com

Red Iguana
✉ Route Touristique, Port El Kantaoui ☎ 096 240250

Jerba and the South

Jerba's climate and beauty are legendary, and the growing number of tourists is starting to clash with the traditional life in the villages. The more remote but definitely gorgeous desert region of Tunisia, covering much of the southern half of the country is, however, less visited.

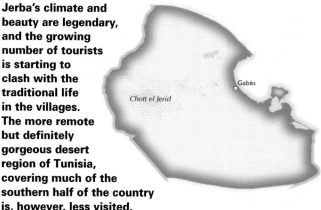

Gabès

Chott el Jerid

The oasis of Tozeur has established itself as the most popular destination in the region. This part of Tunisia offers a fascinating

mix of sand dunes and lush oases and salt lakes in the Jerid, and further south arid mountains with ancient Berber villages and *ksour* (fortified granaries).

European holidaymakers usually prefer to visit the desert region in early spring or late autumn as the summer months can be oppressively hot.

Desert safaris from the east coast beach resorts rarely stay more than two or three nights in the region, with Tozeur the traditional focal point. Popular spots en route include Matmata with its unusual cave dwellings, and the Gorges de Selja, famous for the rail journey on Le Lézard Rouge (Red Lizard) train.

Jerba

Thought to be the 'land of the Lotus Eaters', where Ulysses came ashore during his Odyssey, Jerba has a mild climate for most of the year (although it can be quite chilly from November to January, with temperatures dropping even further at night), but the vegetation is less lush than it must once have been. The land is pretty arid, and only olive trees and Barbarie figs seem to thrive. Jerba is the holiday destination of many Tunisians and Europeans, so much so that the small island has its own international airport and a vast resort strip.

While its population, now 120,000, is one of the most cosmopolitan in the country, Jerba society is deeply conservative and – confronted with the demands of foreign tourists – there remains a strong determination to preserve the island's distinct identity. Just 29km (18 miles) wide by 27km (17 miles) long, Jerba is said to have 354 mosques; one for every day of the Islamic year.

➕ S24 ✉ 506km (314 miles) south of Tunis 🚌 Daily services to Sousse, Sfax and Tunis ✈ Daily flights from Jerba to Tunis from Jerba–Zarzis; international flights

ℹ Place des Martyrs, Houmt Souq ☎ 75 650915

AJIM

Visitors arriving by ferry dock at Ajim. Once an important centre for sponges, which are collected from the seabed by divers, it is now mainly a busy fishing port. In the summer months there can be long queues for the car ferry to El Jorf – a two-hour wait is not unusual. Swimming around Ajim is not recommended, as there are often swarms of jellyfish in this area, as well as octopuses.

➕ R25 ✉ 22km (14 miles) south of Houmt Souq ⛴ To Jorf every 30 minutes, 4am–midnight, every hour midnight–4am ✋ Inexpensive for cars; free for passengers on foot

EL KANTARA CAUSEWAY

Driving across the El Kantara Causeway is the alternative to taking the ferry to and from the mainland, but it adds around 100km (62 miles) to a journey. The first causeway, an impressive feat of engineering, was built in Carthaginian times and survived until 1551, when it was badly damaged by the Turkish pirate Dragut. Repairs were not made until 1953.

✚ S25 ✉ 7km (4 miles) long from southeast corner of Île de Jerba to the mainland ✋ Free

ERRIADH (HARA SEGHIRA)

The only reason to come here is to see the **El Ghriba Synagogue,** one of the most holy Jewish shrines in North Africa. There has been a strong Jewish presence in Tunisia, and particularly in Jerba, for many centuries. Jerba's Jews today number around a thousand, many having migrated to Israel, and the synagogue now provides a meeting place for the ageing community. Suitably dressed visitors may enter the synagogue to see its bright blue pillars, painted tiles and stained glass.

➕ S24 ✉ 8km (5 miles) from Houmt Souq 🚌 Bus No 14 from Houmt Souq to Guellala (➤ below) stop in Erriadh

El Ghriba Synagogue

✉ 1km (half a mile) from town centre ☎ 75 670921 🕓 Sun–Thu 9:30–12:30, 2:30–5, Fri 9:30–2 💰 Inexpensive

GUELLALA

Guellala rivals Nabeul (➤ 118–121) as a pottery-producing centre. The clay for the pottery – all of which is handmade – is quarried

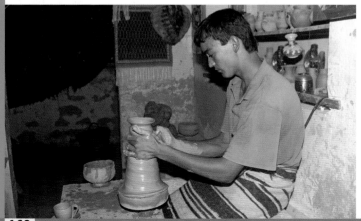

from hills above the village and out towards Sedouikech. The main street is lined with shops piled high with pots and plates, most made in Tozeur or Nabeul. Typical Guellala pottery is handmade, rougher, heavier and rarely glazed. There are many workshops and kilns in the village making traditional household objects. The 'magic camel', a water jug in the shape of a camel, is one of the favourite items for sale. Guellala is a popular morning stop on coach tours of the island, so the best bargains can usually be negotiated in mid-afternoon when there are fewer people around.

The Mosquée de Guellala (1km/half a mile out of town on the road to Erriadh) dates from the 15th century. The Musée de Guellala (1km/half a mile away on the road to Sedouikech) has exhibitions explaining the traditional Tunisian way of life, and includes wedding outfits and domestic scenes.

✚ S25 ✉ 18km (11 miles) from Houmt Souq 🚌 Ten buses (No 14) a day from Houmt Souq

HOUMT SOUQ

Houmt Souq, the capital of Jerba, is situated on the island's north coast, 6km (4 miles) from the airport at Mellita. It is a charming place to spend a few days and makes a good base for excursions to other parts of the island and further afield. Houmt Souq means 'marketplace', and this remains the town's primary purpose despite its now blossoming tourist industry, which has brought the inevitable crop of souvenir shops and European-style restaurants.

The heart of the town is the snug little complex of whitewashed squares and streets surrounding the souq, where goods including jewellery, coral and leatherware are sold. There is also a daily fish auction. Mondays and Thursdays are the busiest days, when traders come in from all over the island to sell straw baskets and mats.

On the seafront, close to Houmt Souq's busy fishing harbour, is the **Borj el Kebir** (also known as Borj Ghazi Mustapha). There has probably been a fort here since Roman times, but the earliest remains are of a fortress built at the end of the 13th century by the Sicilian Roger de Loria. Most

of the existing structure dates from the late 15th and early 16th centuries. In 1560 – when controlled by the Spanish – it was the scene of a famous two-month siege and massacre led by the Turkish pirate Dragut, who stormed the castle and killed all its occupants. The skulls of the defeated Spanish soldiers were dumped in an 11m-high (36ft) pile close to the port; today a small white monument marks the spot.

Among several interesting mosques (all closed to non-Muslims) are the multi-domed Mosque of the Strangers, the Jami'et-Turuk (Mosque of the Turks), which has a beautiful minaret, and the Zaouia de Sidi Brahim, containing the tomb of a 17th-century saint.

The **Musée des Arts et Traditions Populaires** (Museum of Arts and Popular Traditions) is housed in a former mosque, the Zaouia de Sidi Zitouna. Dedicated to Jerban culture, it has a large collection of costumes and jewellery, a reconstruction of a pottery workshop with huge jars which were used to store everything from grain to clothing, and a room full of antique wooden chests.

✚ S24 ✉ 22km (13.5 miles) northeast of Ajim 🍴 Good choice (£–££)

🚌 Bus station on rue Mosbah Jarbou

ℹ Place des Martyrs ✉ 75 650915

Borj el Kebir

✉ At the seafront end of rue Taieb Mehiri, 700m (765yds) from the fishing port ⏰ Sat–Thu 8–7 (9:30–4:30 in winter) 💲 Inexpensive

Musée des Arts et Traditions Populaires

✉ Avenue Abdelhamid el-Kadhi ☎ 75 650540 ⏰ Sat–Thu 8–noon, 3–7 (9:30–4:30 in winter) 💲 Moderate

MIDOUN

Jerba's second biggest town really springs to life on Friday – market day – when streets all around the centre are filled with makeshift stalls, attracting a large crowd of local people and tourists. Try to arrive early because it is all but over by lunchtime. Another crowd puller takes place on Tuesday afternoons (3pm; 5pm Jun–Aug), when a mock Berber wedding procession is held for the benefit of visitors.

➕ S24 ✉ 16km (10 miles) east of Houmt Souq 🍴 Several (£–££)
🚌 Frequent from Houmt Souq and the tourist resorts
ℹ Main square ☎ 75 658074

SIDI MAHREZ

Starting at Flamingo Point, about 8km (5 miles) east of Houmt
Souq, and extending as far as Ras Taguermes (marked by a
lighthouse), this 10km (6-mile) stretch of coastline is said to be the
best beach in Jerba. The *zone touristique* occupies some of this
with its cluster of large hotels, but there are also quieter areas.

   Another unspoiled stretch can be found south of Aghir, while
the wild and rocky west coast is almost totally uninhabited.

➕ S24 ✉ 8–18km (5–11 miles) east of Houmt Souq 🍴 Bar snacks at the
beach hotels 🚌 Bus from Houmt Souq

More to see in the South

CHEBIKA

Chebika is the southernmost of three mountain villages
close to the Algerian border which can be visited together
on a day trip from Tozeur (▶ 176–181). The others are
Midès (▶ 173) and Tamerza (▶ 174–175).

Abandoned after serious flooding in 1969, the old village
of Chebika is now in ruins, but the villagers are making the
most of tourism. Guides will lead you up the mountainside
to see the waterfall which feeds the oasis; there is a good
view of the salt lake of Chott el Gharsa.

✚ J13 ✉ 60km (37 miles) northwest of Tozeur 🚌 No public
transport; join an organized excursion or rent a car

CHOTT EL JERID

Chott el Jerid is the most southwesterly of a series of salt
lakes lying inland of Gabès (▶ 170). This vast salt lake of shifting
colours and mirages covers nearly 5,000sq km (1,930sq miles).
Lifeless in summer, the water evaporates leaving a crust of salt
crystals which glisten in the sun: brilliant white interspersed with
patches of green, orange and pink, caused by the different
chemical constituents of the salts. In winter water collects on
either side of the raised causeway built across the Chott from
Degache to Kebili (▶ 182–183) and life returns to this inland sea.

The lake is fringed with small oasis towns, whose economy depends entirely on the cultivation of dates.

Journeys across the Chott used to be hazardous and all the tourist literature tells of a huge caravan wandering off the main route and disappearing through the thin surface. It's still advised not to go off the beaten track.

➕ K15 ✉ Kebili is 120km (75 miles) west of Gabès 🍽 Small cafés in most oasis towns 🚌 Four a day from Gabès

DOUZ

Douz is right on the edge of the desert, as most northerners think of it. The dunes are not quite so impressive here as they are a bit deeper into the Eastern Desert but they are real enough to satisfy most visitors. Just outside the town near the village of Gleissia is the Great Dune, where most tours stop. The town centre is transformed early on a Thursday morning into a frenetic weekly produce market which draws shoppers and traders from a wide area, selling everything from sheep, goats and camels, to dates, spices and beans, as well as clothing and leather goods.

The small but interesting **Douz Museum of the Sahara** explores the history and culture of the southern Jerid, and has costumes, jewellery, camel harnesses and a Bedouin tent.

➕ L16 ✉ 148km (92 miles) southwest of Gabès 🍽 Choice of cafés (£) 🚌 To Tunis, Tozeur, Sfax, Gabès, Kebili and Matmata
ℹ Avenue des Martyrs ☎ 75 470351
🕐 Daily 8–1, 3–6

Douz Museum of the Sahara

✉ Avenue des Martyrs 🕐 Tue–Sun 9–12, 3–5 (9:30–4:30 in winter) 🖐 Inexpensive

GABÈS

Initially Gabès may appear to be a modern industrial city at the crossroads for tours to the interior, but it has more to offer. It was a major Phoenician and Roman port; during the 14th century it was on the main east–west trading route and was a transit stop for Muslim pilgrims en route to Mecca. It was heavily battered in World War II raids and by devastating floods in 1962, but the old town still has atmosphere with its souq and mosques. Its huge plantation of date palms is a true oasis.

➕ Q24 ✉ 405km (250 miles) south of Tunis 🍴 Wide choice of restaurants (£–££) 🚆 To Sfax, Sousse and Tunis 🚌 To Matmata, Tunis, Jerba, Douz, Kebili and Tataouine 🛈 Place de la Liberté ☎ 75 272577

GAFSA

A former Berber stronghold and prosperous Roman town, Gafsa is an important regional centre and phosphate-producing town. Most tourists pass through on their way to the salt lakes and dunes but there is a picturesque kasbah, a huge date palm grove and Piscines Romaines (Roman Pools) with a small museum.

➕ L13 ✉ 93km (58 miles) northeast of Tozeur 🍴 Good choice (£–££) 🚌 To Tunis, Tozeur, Nefta, Gabès, Sfax and Sousse 🛈 Place des Piscines Romaines ☎ 76 221664

GORGES DE SELJA

This impressive 15km-long (9-mile) gorge stretches from Redeyef to Metlaoui, a thriving phosphate mining town. One of the best ways to see the gorge is from **Le Lézard Rouge** (the Red Lizard), a restored 19th-century train which operates a two-hour round-trip from Metlaoui. Selja itself is halfway along the gorge and is a good place to stop for a walk down into the deepest parts of the gorge. The railway tunnels and bridges were originally built by the French to transport phosphate from the mines to Gafsa (➤ opposite).

✚ K13 ✉ 16km (10 miles) west of Metlaoui ⏹ Le Lézard Rouge ✉ Metlaoui station ☎ 76 241469; one departure a day ✋ Expensive

KSAR OULED SOLTANE

Best places to see, ➤ 46–47.

MATMATA

This is one of the best-known villages in Tunisia, due to the opening sequence of the original *Star Wars* movie, which featured its troglodyte dwellings. Dating from the 4th century BC, many of the underground houses are still inhabited, providing homes that are cool in summer and warm in winter. Some of the houses can be visited by arrangement with the owners, but it is advisable to agree a price beforehand or buy some of the craft goods on sale. Three of the troglodyte dwellings in Old Matmata have been turned into hotels: the Marhala, part of a chain run by the Touring Club de Tunisie; the Hôtel Sidi Driss, whose bar also appeared in the film as the setting for the alien jazz club sequence; and Les Berbères – named after the people who have lived here for centuries.

✚ Q25 ✉ 43km (27 miles) southwest of Gabès ✋ By arrangement
🍴 Hôtel Marhala ☎ 75 240015; Hôtel Sidi Driss ☎ 75 240005; Hôtel Berbères ☎ 75 240024 🚌 Up to ten buses a day to Gabès and daily services to Jerba, Douz, Sfax, Sousse, Tamezret and Tunis
ℹ Main square ☎ 75 240114

MEDENINE

Since 1800, Medenine has grown rapidly in importance, becoming one of the main cities in the south. Its weekly market on Sunday attracts people from all over the region. At some point its *ksar* (granary), which belonged to the Touazine and Khezour tribes, had more than 8,000 *ghorfas* (stone rooms).

On a quest for modernity the local authorities destroyed most of the five or six top floors of the large *ksar*, and the remaining ground floor has unfortunately become something of a tourist trap, with almost all the *ghorfas* now souvenir shops. The best

time to visit, therefore, is at night when the shops have closed. A short bus ride away is the much better preserved 600-year-old *ksar* of Metameur. It is much smaller, with three storeys of *ghorfas* around three courtyards, one of which is now a hotel.

🚹 R26 ✉ 60km (37 miles) from Zarzis 🚌 Two or three buses a day to Gabès, Jerba, Tataouine, Tunis and Douz 🍴 Le Carthage (£), rue du 18 Janvier ❓ Festival of El Jezz, end of May–early Jun

MIDÈS

The oasis village of Midès is in the mountains which border Algeria. Originally a Berber village, Midès became an outpost of the Roman Empire. All but a handful of residents have now left their single room mud-brick houses in the original village, perched precariously on the sides of the deep gorge, and moved to the new town, which has been built on the other side of the palm grove. The oasis itself is, as usual, a place of refuge from the fierce heat of this desert region. The Tunisian government is now helping to restore the old houses as tourist accommodation and shops selling local produce and souvenirs to a small but steadily increasing stream of day-trippers.

🚹 J13 ✉ 75km (46 miles) west of Gafsa 🚌 None; join an organized excursion or rent a car

NEFTA

Best places to see, ➤ 50–51.

REMADA

Remada, Tunisia's southernmost town, beyond which there is nothing but desert, is dominated by the military, due to the proximity of the Libyan border. Centred on a little oasis where the Romans had a small fort, daily life focuses on the shady place de l'Indépendence. Remada's most distinctive sight is on the southern edge of town – a 15-domed mud-brick building once used as a slaughterhouse. Borg Bourguiba, 40km (25 miles) southwest of Remada, is where Habib Bourguiba was held prisoner for a year in the early 1950s.

➕ Q28 (off map) ✉ 70km (43 miles) south of Tataouine 🚌 Daily from Tataouine 🍴 Cafés (£) on place de l'Indépendence

TAMERZA

Once a Roman military post called Ad Turres, Tamerza later became the seat of a Christian bishop during the Byzantine era. The original village of Tamerza was devastated by catastrophic

flooding in 1969 and now lies abandoned. Today visitors walk through its eerily empty streets; it looks strangely beautiful at night when floodlit and viewed from the comfort of the Tamerza Palace Hotel, directly opposite. There is a small waterfall and a swimming area known as the Cascades.

➕ J13 ✉ 85km (53 miles) west of Gafsa
🍴 Le Soleil (➤ 186) ☎ 76 485344
🚌 Daily buses to Tunis and Gafsa
ℹ Tourist bureau on main road
✉ 76 485288 🕐 Daily 8–1, 3–6

TATAOUINE

A good base for exploring the *ksour* or fortified villages (➤ 46–47). *Tataouine* is a Berber word meaning 'springs' and historically there was an important camel market here. A busy market is still held here every Monday and

Thursday, in and around the central souq. One of the most picturesque in the region, it is among the best places to buy *kilims* (woven rugs) and pottery. Ksar Megabla, 2km (1.2 miles) south of the town centre, offers good views of the surrounding area.

➕ R27 ✉ 49km (30 miles) south of Medenine 🍴 Hôtel Sangho (££)
✉ 3km (2 miles) from town on road to Chenini ☎ 75 860102 🚌 To Sfax, Sousse, Gabès, Jerba and Tunis ℹ Avenue Habib Bourguiba ☎ 75 850686
❓ Festival of the Ksour, Mar; Festival of Shearing the Camels, Apr

TOZEUR

The area around Tozeur has been inhabited since at least 8000BC, sited around an oasis on the northern shore of the great salt lake of Chott el Jerid. The town prospered as a trading post on the route of the great trans-Saharan caravans, but today Tozeur is the focal point of Tunisia's ever-expanding desert tourist industry. Once merely an overnight stop on desert safaris from the east coast resorts, today Tozeur is an established resort in its own right.

➕ J14 ✉ 220km (138 miles) west of Gabès
🍴 Choice (£–£££) around avenue Bourguiba
🚌 To Tunis, Nefta, Gafsa and Kebili 🚆 Twice daily to Sfax, Tunis, Gafsa and Sousse ✈ Regular flights to Tunis, Jerba and Monastir; also international flights ❓ Festival International des Oasis, Dec
ℹ Avenue Abdul Kacem Chebbi ☎ 76 454088

Belvédère

This rocky outcrop offers panoramic views over the palm grove (➤ 180), the Chott el Jerid (➤ 168–169) and the Chott el Gharsa. It is a 20-minute walk from the Dar Cheraït Museum (➤ below); go early in the morning, at sunset, or at night when it is floodlit.
✉ 3km (2 miles) southwest of the town centre 🕐 Open access ✋ Free

Dar Cheraït Museum

Purpose-built in the style of an upper-class Tunis town house, the museum's displays depict scenes from Tunisian life past and present: there is a typical kitchen, a *bey's* bedroom, a wedding scene, a hammam and a Bedouin tent. There are displays of costumes, jewellery, ceramics and sacred books; and the work

of weavers, cobblers and tailors is also highlighted. A sound-and-light show called 'One Thousand and One Nights' is based (very) loosely on the book of the same name.

www.darcherait.com.tn

✉ Route Touristique ☎ 76 452100 ⊕ 8am–midnight ✋ Moderate

a walk around Tozeur

This walk combines Tozeur's busy central thoroughfare with a glimpse of the palmery.

Start at the Grand Hôtel de l'Oasis and walk up avenue Habib Bourguiba.

Tozeur's main street is a curious mix of sleepy desert town, catering for the everyday needs of local people, and brash tourist centre with dozens of shops selling carpets, pottery and stuffed camels.

At the tiered pottery bowl landmark turn right for a look around Tozeur's covered market hall. Walk past the slim sandstone minaret of Mosquée El Farkous, turning right at the end of avenue Habib Bourguiba. Continue straight ahead at place des Martyrs. Take the second right towards Mosquée Sidi Abdesallem at the far end. Veer left towards a dome-shaped tiled monument in front of the École Primaire ibn Chabbat and walk down the left-hand side of the school. After 200m (220yds), at the end of

a concrete wall, turn right following the path through a courtyard to the palmery.

Tozeur's palmery (➤ 180), covering around 10sq km (4sq miles), has more than 200,000 palm trees and 200 springs.

After two or three minutes' walk, cross a small stream, turn left out of the palmery and then right following a path leading into the médina. Take the third turning right, under a double arch. Note the roofs made of dried palm trunks.

Call in at the Musée des Arts et Traditions Populaires (➤ 180).

Turn right out of the museum. At the end of the street, turn left, which leads back to avenue Habib Bourguiba.

Distance 5km (3 miles)
Time Half a day allowing for visits
Start/end point Grand Hôtel de l'Oasis ✉ Place des Martyrs
☎ 76 452699
Drinks Cafés (£) on avenue Habib Bourguiba

Musée des Arts et Traditions Populaires

The Museum of Arts and Popular Traditions illustrates the traditional way of life. One of the most interesting exhibits is a collection of manuscripts describing Tozeur's water system. Originally conceived in the 13th century by the town's *imam* (religious leader) Ibn Chabbat, the distribution network was handed down orally from generation to generation until finally committed to paper in 1911.

✉ Rue de Kairouan ⏰ Tue–Sun 8–12, 3–6 (4–7 in summer) 🖐 Inexpensive

Ouled el Hadef

Tozeur's Old Town is a web of narrow alleys, changed little since the 14th century when it was built by the Ouled el Hadef tribe. Its distinctive architecture is considered to be one of the marvels of Islamic art. Unique to Tozeur and neighbouring Nefta (► 50–51), houses are decorated with geometric motifs (also found on local carpets and shawls). The yellowish bricks are handmade from a mix of local sand and clay and provide excellent insulation against the extremes of the desert climate, swelteringly hot in summer and freezing on winter nights.

✉ North and east of the Hôtel Splendid 🍴 Choice of cafés (£) 🖐 Free

Palmery

Within the oasis at Tozeur are hundreds of thousands of date palms and more than 200 springs. The palmery is best viewed from the Belvédère (► 176) or from a *calèche* (horse-drawn carriage), which you can rent to drive around the palm groves. A popular stop is Le Paradis, a lush tropical garden with a small zoo, 3km (2 miles) from the centre (daily 7:30–sunset).

✉ Northeast of the Market Square 🚌 *Calèches* for rent from opposite the Hôtel Karim ⏰ Open access 🖐 Free

from Tozeur to Kebili: the road across the Chott

A drive along the causeway across the Chott el Jerid, which can produce stunning mirages.

Leave Tozeur heading northeast on the 3. After 8km (5 miles), drive through the village of Bouhel, turn right and 3km (2 miles) later pass through Degache, which marks the start of the 80km-long/2m-high (50-mile/6ft) causeway across the Chott.

The Chott el Jerid (➤ 168–169) is one of a series of giant salt lakes that divide the north of the country from the true desert landscape of the south. There are no significant landmarks en route; however, look out for the abandoned burnt-out shell of a bus and a handful of isolated huts and stalls selling souvenirs. The terrain can appear to change enormously according to the time of year and the brightness of the sunshine. In winter if there has been quite a lot of rain it is not unusual for the water to look pink

on one side of the road and green on the other; this is caused by the natural chemicals in the water.

The first signs of life come as you pass through the village of Souq Lahad, which is worth a short stop. You reach Kebili after another 15km (9 miles).

Kebili was an important slave-trading town until the 19th century, but is now a regional transport centre. There is a large palm grove, and just outside town, a Roman bathing pool and hammam fed by a 3km-deep (2-mile) borehole.

Leave Kebili, returning to Tozeur along the causeway.

Distance 186km (115 miles)
Time Allow five hours, including time for lunch and a bathe in the Roman pool
Start/end point Tozeur ✚ J14
Lunch Hôtel l'Oasis dar Kebili (££–£££) ✉ Zone Touristique de Kebili ☎ 75 491436

HOTELS

DOUZ
Méhari Douz (£££)
The fortress-like Méhari is one of the more established hotels in
Douz, with small but comfortable rooms around a bright courtyard.
✉ Zone Touristique ☎ 75 471088; www.goldenyasmin.com

GABÈS
Atlantic (£)
A once-grand colonial-style hotel, now long past its best, but still
with some character.
✉ 4 avenue Habib Bourguiba ☎ 75 220034

JERBA
Dar Faïza (£)
See page 74.

Erriadh (£)
This delightful *fondouk* in the heart of Houmt Souq, built around
a vine-covered courtyard, oozes charm and character.
✉ 10 rue Mohamed Ferjani, Houmt Souq ☎ 75 650756

Sables d'Or (£)
Converted house with a central patio in the centre of Houmt Souq.
The 12 rooms are kept spotlessly clean and all have showers – but
there are communal toilets.
✉ 30 rue Mohammed Ferjani, Houmt Souq ☎ 75 650423

MATMATA
Marhala (£)
See page 75.

NEFTA
Marhala (£–££)
This former brick factory on the edge of Nefta's oasis is now a
hotel run by the Touring Club de Tunisie. Swimming pool.
✉ Route Touristique ☎ 76 430027

TAMERZA
Tamerza Palace Hotel (££–£££)
See page 75.

TOZEUR
Grand Hotel de L'Oasis (££)
Centrally located hotel popular with tourists on desert safaris. The rooms are a bit like cells but the service is friendly and there is a decent bar and restaurant.
✉ Avenue Aboul Kacem Chebbi ☎ 76 452300

Ksar Rouge (££–£££)
Elegant and very luxurious hotel in local architectural style, with several pools, a sauna and a gym.
✉ Beginning of the Route Touristique ☎ 76 454933

RESTAURANTS

GABÈS
Restaurant de l'Oasis (££)
This old-fashioned French-Tunisian restaurant is generally reckoned to be the top spot in Gabès. The set menu is good value.
✉ 17 avenue Farhat Hached ☎ 75 270098 🕓 Lunch, dinner

JERBA
El Foundouk (££)
Intimate and cosy restaurant in the shade of an old tree. Very good Tunisian specialities.
✉ Avenue Habib Bourguiba, Houmt Souq ☎ 75 653238 🕓 Lunch, dinner

Le Moulin (££)
Renowned for its simple, fresh, well-prepared cuisine, Le Moulin serves mainly Tunisian specialities, fish and seafood in a very relaxed atmosphere
✉ Zone Touristique ☎ 75 758336 🕓 Lunch, dinner

La Princesse d'Haroun (£££)

Jerba's most famous restaurant. In summer you can eat on the terrace overlooking the harbour. Meat dishes available, but seafood starters and grilled fish rule. Smart casual dress preferred.

✉ Opposite the fishing harbour ☎ 75 650488 🕐 Lunch, dinner

TAMERZA

Le Soleil (£–££)

Attractive restaurant in an old house near the mosque, serving delicious, home-cooked Tunisian dishes.

✉ Close to the mosque ☎ No phone 🕐 Lunch, dinner

TOZEUR

Azzurra (£)

Pizzeria with an outdoor terrace, serving great pizzas, sandwiches and salads, perfect for a light lunch or dinner. No alcohol.

✉ Opposite Dar Cheraït Museum, Route Touristique ☎ 76 463082 🕐 Daily 9am–10pm

Le Petit Prince (££)

Long-established restaurant which sometimes has evening shows of traditional music and dancing.

✉ Off avenue Abou el Kacem Chabbi ☎ 76 452518 🕐 Dinner

Restaurant de la République (£)

Tucked away in a corner, this cosy little restaurant appeals to local people and tourists. Good, affordable food.

✉ Avenue Habib Bourguiba (back of an arcade of shops) 🕐 Lunch, dinner

Le Soleil (£)

Opposite Résidence Warda, the best of Tozeur's budget options with clean surroundings and an extensive menu. Camel-meat couscous is available if ordered in advance.

✉ Avenue Abou el Kacem Chabbi ☎ 76 554220 🕐 Lunch, dinner

Sight Locator Index

This index relates to the maps on the covers. We have given map references to the main sights of interest in the book. Grid references in italics indicate sights featured on the town plan. Some sights within towns may not be plotted on the maps.

Ajim **R25**

Avenue Habib Bourguiba *Tunis g3*

Béja **L6**

Bizerte **C1**

Bulla Regia **K6**

Carthage **D3**

Cathédrale de St Vincente de Paul *Tunis f3*

Chebika **J13**

Chott el Jerid **K15**

Dougga **L7**

Douz **L16**

El Haouaria **F2**

El Jem **R20**

El Kantara Causeway **S25**

El Kef **K8**

Erriadh (Hara Seghira) **S24**

Gabès **Q24**

Gafsa **L13**

Gammarth **D2**

Gorges de Selja **K13**

Guellala **S25**

Hammamet **E4**

Houmt Souq **S24**

Îles Kerkennah **S22**

Jebel Ichkeul National Park (Parc National de l'Ichkeul) **B1**

Jemaa ez Zitouna *Tunis c4*

Jerba **S24**

Kairouan **Q19**

Kélibia **F2**

Kerkouane **F2**

Korbous **E3**

Ksar Ouled Soltane **R28**

La Goulette **D3**

La Marsa **D2**

Mahdia **S19**

Matmata **Q25**

Medenine **R26**

Médina *Tunis c3*

Midès **J13**

Midoun **S24**

Monastir **R18**

Musée des Arts Populaires et Traditions *Tunis d5*

Musée du Bardo **C3** or *Tunis b1* **(off map)**

Nabeul **E4**

Nefta **H15**

Parc du Belvédère *Tunis f1* **(off map)**

Port el Kantoui **R18**

Remada **Q28 (off map)**

Sbeïtla **L10**

Sfax **R22**

Sidi Bou Saïd **D2**

Sidi Mahrez **S24**

Souqs *Tunis c4*

Sousse **R18**

Tabarka **K5**

Tamerza **J13**

Tataouine **R27**

Thermes d'Antonin **D3**

Thuburbo Majus **C4**

Thuburnica **K6**

Tozeur **J14**

Tunis **D3**

Utique (Utica) **C2**

Zaghouan **D4**

Index

accommodation 74–75, 106–108, 126–128, 155–157, 184–185
Acqua Palace 63
activities 66
Aghlabid Pools 45
Aïn el Kef 144
air travel 26, 28
Ajim 160
American War Cemetery 87
amusement parks 62–63
Antonine Baths 54–55, 72
Archaeological Museum, El Jem 39
Archaeological Museum, Mahdia 146–147
Archaeological Museum, Sfax 153
archaeological sites 72
Association de Sauvegarde de Médina 140
Avenue Habib Bourguiba, Tunis 80–81

Bab el Bahr 83
banks 30
Bassins des Aglabides 45
Béja 95
Belvédère, Tozeur 176
Beni Khiar 121
Bizerte 79, 96–97, 105
Borj el Kebir, Houmt Souq 164–165
Borj el Kebir, Mahdia 147, 148
Borj el-Hissar 40
Borg Bourguiba 174
Bourguiba, Habib 40, 82, 174
Bourguiba Mausolée 140
breakdowns 27
Bulla Regia 72, 98
buses 28
Byrsa Hill 87

café terraces 64
Camel Market, Nabeul 118
camels 18, 66, 118
Cap Bon 111–130
car rental 29
carpets 71
Carthage 72, 86–91
Carthageland 62
catacombs 132
Cathédrale de St Louis 87
Cathédrale de St Vincente de Paul 81
Cave of the Bats 116, 124
central Tunisia 131–158

Centre for Arab and Mediterranean Music 52, 53
Centre International Culturel 112–113
Chebika 168
Chergui 40
children's attractions 62–63
Chott el Gharsa 78, 168, 176
Chott el Jerid 78, 168–169, 176, 182–183
climate and seasons 11, 22, 31–32
credit cards 30
currency and exchange 30
cycling 66

Dar Cheraït Museum 176–177
Dar Hammamet 113
Dar Othman 69, 83
dental services 23
desert region 159
diving 66
Dougga 36–37, 72
Douz 18, 169
Douz Museum of the Sahara 169
drink driving 27
drives
    around Cap Bon 124–125
    Sousse to El Jem 138–139
    Tozeur to Kebili 182–183
    Tunis to Lac Ichkeul 104–105
driving 22, 27

eating out 58–59, 60, 64, 108–110, 128–130, 157–158, 185–186
El Ghriba Synagogue 162
El Haouaria 116, 124
El Jem 38–39, 72, 138–139
El Kantara Causeway 161
El Kef 144–145
electricity 31
embassies and consulates 31
emergency telephone numbers 31
entertainment 110, 130, 158
Erriadh (Hara Seghira) 162

fares and tickets 29
ferries 26
Ferryville 104
festivals and events 24–25
fishing 66
food and drink 12–15, 17, 18, 71, see also eating out
Fort d'Espagne 97
four-wheel driving 66

Friguia Animal Park 62
fuel 27

Gabès 170
Gafsa 170
Gammarth 92
geography 11
Ghar el Kebir 116, 124
Gharbi 40
golf 66
Gorges de Selja 159, 171
Grande Bain Maure Sidi Bouraoui 132–133
Grande Mosquée, Sousse 134
Grande Mosquée de Sidi Oqba 44, 45
Great Dune 169
Great Mosque, Bizerte 97
Great Mosque, Kairouan 44, 45
Great Mosque, Sfax 154
Great Mosque, Sousse 134
Great Mosque, Tunis 68, 82
Guellala 17, 162–163

Hammamet 111, 112–115
hammams (Turkish baths) 132–133, 137
Hara Seghira 162
health advice 22, 23, 31–32
Houmt Souq 70, 164–165

Îles Kerkennah 40–41
insurance 22, 23
internet services 31

Jami'et-Turuk 165
Jebel Ichkeul National Park 42–43
Jebel Khawi 92
Jemaa ez Zitouna 68, 82
Jerba 159, 160–167
jewellery 71

Kairouan 44–45, 70, 131
kasbah, Hammamet 114
Kasbah Sousse Museum 134–135
kasbah, El Kef 144, 145
Kebili 183
Kélibia 116, 124
Kerkouane 72, 117, 124
Korba 124
Korbous 118
Ksar Hallouf 47
Ksar Megabla 175
Ksar Ouled Soltane 46–47

La Goulette 92–93
La Grotte des Chauves-Souris 116
La Marsa 93
language 11, 33
Le Lézard Rouge 159, 171
Les Aiguilles (The Needles) 101
Les Ports Puniques 88

Magon Quarter, Carthage 90
Mahdia 131, 146–147
Mansoura 116, 124
Marché Central, Nabeul 118
markets 70, 118
Matmata 18, 72, 159, 172
Medenine 172–173
médina, Hammamet 114–115
médina, Monastir 140
médina, Sfax 154
médina, Sousse 135
médina, Tunis 16, 68–69, 83
Metameur 47
Midès 173
Midoun 166–167
Moknine 139
Monastir 131, 138, 139, 140–143
money 30
Mosquée de Guellala 163
Mosquée de Hammouda Pacha 83
Mosquée Sidi Youssef 83
Mosquée des Trois Portes 44
Musée des Arts et Traditions
   Populaires, Jerba 165
Musée des Arts et Traditions
   Populaires, Tozeur 179, 180
Musée des Arts Populaires et
   Traditions, Tunis 84
Musée du Bardo, Tunis 48–49
Musée du Costume Traditionnel
   142
Musée de Guellala 163
Musée de Kalaout el Koubba 137
Musée National de Carthage 89
Musée Oceanographique, Bizerte
   97
Musée Oceanographique,
   Carthage 90
Musée des Ports Puniques 88
Musée Régional, Nabeul 119, 121
Musée Régional des Arts et
   Traditions, Sfax 154
Musée Regional des Arts et
   Traditions Populaires, El Kef 145
Musée Romain et Paléo-Chrétien
   89
Museum of Islamic Arts 142–143

Nabeul 17, 70, 111, 118–121, 124
national holidays 24
Neapolis 119, 121
Nefta 50–51
nightlife 110, 130, 158
northern Tunisia 79–110

Oceanographic Museum, Bizerte
   97
opening hours 32
Ouled el Hadef 180

Palmery 179, 180
Parc Archéologique des Villas
   Romaines 90
Parc du Belvédère 84
Parc National de l'Ichkeul 42–43
passports and visas 22
personal safety 32
pharmacies 32
picnic spots 60
police 31
population 11
Port El Kantaoui 138, 150–151
postal services 30–31
pottery 16–17, 71, 121, 162–163
public transport 28–29
Puppet 115

Quartier Magon, Carthage 90

Ramadan 24
Red Lizard train 159, 171
Remada 174
Remla 40
ribat, Monastir 139, 142–143
ribat, Sousse 135, 137
Roman Caves 116
Roman and Palaeo-Christian
   Museum 89

Sahel 131
sailing 66
salt lakes 168–169, 182–183
Sanctuary of Tophet 90
sand-skiing 66
Sbeïtla 72, 131, 151
seat belts 27
Sfax 131, 152–154
shopping 70–71
Sidi Bou Saïd 52–53
Sidi Bouraoui Baths 132–133
Sidi Mahrez 167
Souq Lahad 183
souqs 70

souqs, Tunis 85
Sousse 70, 131, 132–137,
   138–139
the south 159–186
souvenirs 71
Spanish Fort, Bizerte 97
speed limits 27
sport 66–67
sun precautions 31

Tabarka 79, 100–101
Tamerza 174–175
Tataouine 46, 175
taxis 29
telephones 31
Tell 131
Temple des Eaux 123
Théâtre d'Hadrien 90
Thermes d'Antonin 54–55, 72
Thuburbo Majus 72, 122–123
Thuburnica 103
time differences 23
Tinja 104
tipping 30
Tourbet el Bey 69, 83
tourist offices 23, 30
Tozeur 159, 176–181, 182
trains 28
trams (métro leger) 28–29
travel documents 22
troglodyte dwellings 172
Tunis 48–49, 68–69, 70, 79, 80–85
Tunnels Reef 100

urban transport 28–29
Utique (Utica) 72, 103, 105

walks
   Mahdia 148–149
   Tozeur 178–179
   Tunis médina 68–69
water sports 66
websites 23
wild birds 42–43
wines 15
woodwork and metalwork 71

Zaghouan 123
Zaouia de Sidi Brahim 50, 165
Zaouia de Sidi Mokhtar 97
Zaouia de Sidi Sahab 44
Zoo du Belvédère 63, 84

Acknowledgements

The Automobile Association would like to thank the following photographers and companies for their assistance in the preparation of this book.

Abbreviations for the picture credits are as follows – (t) top; (b) bottom; (c) centre; (l) left; (r) right; (AA) AA World Travel Library.

4l Monastir, AA/S Day; **4c** Scenery near Guermessa, AA/S Day; **4r** El Jem, AA/S Day; **5l** Houmt Souq, AA/S Day; **5c** Cathedral and National Museum of Carthage, Byrsa Hill, AA/S Day; **6/7** Monastir, AA/S Day; **8/9** Temple des Nymphes, Zaghouan, AA/S Day; **10/11t** Rue Kheireddine, Béja, AA/S Day; **10bl** Sidi Bou Saïd, AA/S Day; **10br** Arab horseman, Douz, AA/S Day; **11bl** Corinthian columns, Capitol, Dougga, AA/S Day; **12bl** Market, Douz, AA/S Day; **12br** Chillies, Douz, AA/S Day; **13t** Market, Tunis, AA/S Day; **13b** Café de Paris, Avenue Habib Bourguiba, Tunis, AA/S Day; **14** Thursday market, Douz, AA/S Day; **15t** Pomegranates, AA/S Day; **15b** Buffet, Monastir, AA/S Day; **16b** Carpets, Houmt Souq, AA/S Day; **17t** Guellala pottery, AA/S Day; **17br** Jasmine for sale, Hammamet, AA/S Day; **18c** Douz National Sahara Festival, AA/S Day; **18bl** Hammam, Tunis, AA/S Day; **18br** Dates, La Corbeille, Nefta, AA/S Day; **19** Sidi Bou Saïd, AA/S Day; **20/21** Scenery near Guermessa, AA/S Day; **24** Drummers, Douz National Sahara Festival, AA/S Day; **25** Cavalry Festival, Kairouan, AA/S Day; **26** Ferry near Sidi Youssef, Kerkennah Isles, AA/S Day; **27** Road between Tunis and Kairouan, AA/S Day; **28/29t** Road near El Kef, AA/S Day; **28b** La Marsa station, AA/S Day; **29b** Tamerza Palace Hotel, AA/S Day; **32t** Policemen, Sousse, AA/S Day; **34/35** Amphitheatre, El Jem, AA/S Day; **36/37** Capitol, Dougga, AA/S Day; **36bl** Theatre, Dougga, AA/S Day; **38tl** El Jem, AA/S Day; **39** El Jem, AA/S Day; **40** Look-out tower, Kerkennah Isles, AA/S Day; **41** Kerkannah Isles, AA/S Day; **42/43b** Lake Ichkeul, AA/S Day; **43t** Purple Gallinule, AA/S Day; **44l** Kairouan, AA/S Day; **44/45b** Mosque of Sidi Oqba (Great Mosque), Kairouan, AA/S Day; **45t** Carpet shop, Kairouan, AA/S Day; **46/47** Ksar Ouled Soltane, AA/S Day; **48l** Triumph of Neptune mosaic, Musée du Bardo, AA/S Day; **48/49** Ceramics, Musée du Bardo, AA/S Day; **49tr** Mosaic of Ulysses tied to the mast, from El Djem, Musée du Bardo, AA/S Day; **50/51t** Date palms, Corbeille, Nefta, AA/S Day; **50/51b** Palms, Corbeille, Nefta, AA/S Day; **52cl** Sidi Bou Saïd, AA/S Day; **52b** Sidi Bou Saïd and the Gulf of Tunis, AA/S Day; **53** Sidi Bou Saïd, AA/S Day; **54** Thermes d'Antonin, Carthage, AA/S Day; **55t** Thermes d'Antonin, Carthage, AA/S Day; **56/57** Café, Houmt Souq, AA/S Day; **58** Houmt Souq, AA/S Day; **60/61** Balad al-Jerid, Tamerza, AA/S Day; **62/63** Acqua Palace, Port El Kantaoui, The Tunisian National Tourist Office; **65** Café des Nattes, Sidi Bou Saïd, AA/S Day; **66/67** Beach, Sidi Mahares, AA/S Day; **68/69** Courtyard, Dar Ben Abdullah, Tunis, AA/S Day; **69** Zitouna mosque, Tunis, AA/S Day; **70/71** Market, Jemaa ez Zitouna, Tunis, AA/S Day; **72/73** Hip-bath, Kerkouane, AA/S Day; **75** Tamerza Palace Hotel, AA/S Day; **76/77** Cathedral and National Museum of Carthage, Byrsa Hill, AA/S Day; **79** Municipal Theatre, Avenue Habib Bourguiba, Tunis, AA/S Day; **80** Cathedral of St Vincent de Paul, Avenue Habib Bourguiba, Tunis, AA/S Day; **80/81** Avenue Habib Bourguiba, Tunis, AA/S Day; **82/83** Zitouna Mosque, Tunis, AA/S Day; **83br** Hammouda Pacha Mosque, Tunis, AA/S Day; **84l** Dar Ben Abdallah, Tunis, AA/S Day; **84c** Courtyard, Dar Ben Abdullah, Tunis, AA/S Day; **85t** Perfume seller, Tunis, AA/S Day; **85b** Souq el Attarine, Tunis, AA/S Day; **86/87** Cathédrale de St Louis on Byrsa Hill, AA/S Day; **87** Cathédrale de St Louis on Byrsa Hill, AA/S Day; **88bl** Roman sculpture of Silenus and Maenad, Musée National de Carthage, AA/S Day; **88/89** Musée National de Carthage, AA/S Day; **89r** Mosaic depicting a satyr, Musée National de Carthage, AA/S Day; **90b** Tophet, AA/S Day; **90/91** Tophet, AA/S Day; **92** La Goulette, AA/S Day; **93** La Marsa, AA/S Day; **94/95** Rue Kheireddine, Béja, AA/S Day; **95** French colonial church, Béja, AA/S Day; **96** Bizerte, AA/S Day; **97** Bizerte, AA/S Day; **98** Mosaic, House of the Hunt, Bulla Regia, AA/S Day; **99** Bulla Regia, AA/S Day; **100/101t** Tabarka, AA/S Day; **100b** Statue of the former Tunisian leader Habib Bourguiba, Tabarka, AA/S Day; **102** Utica, AA/S Day; **104/105b** Bizerte, AA/S Day; **105t** Wild flowers, Lake Ichkeul, AA/S Day; **105br** Roman city of Utica, AA/S Day; **111** Kasbah, Hammamet, AA/S Day; **112/113** Centre International Culturel, Hammamet, AA/S Day; **113tr** Garden of the Centre International Culturel, Hammamet, AA/S Day; **113cr** Centre International Culturel, Hammamet, AA/S Day; **114/115t** Hammamet seen from the Kasbah, AA/S Day; **115br** Hammamet, AA/S Day; **116/117** Ghar el Kebir, El Haouaria, AA/S Day; **117br** Kerkouane, AA/S Day; **118** Aïn el-Atrous, Korbous, AA/S Day; **119** Pottery shop, Nabeul, AA/S Day; **120/121** Pottery shop, Nabeul, AA/S Day; **122/123** Thuburbo Majus, AA/S Day; **123cr** Mosque of Sidi Azouz, Zaghouan, AA/S Day; **124/125** Ghar el Kebir caves, AA/S Day; **131** Mosque of Sidi Bou Makhlouf, El Kef, AA/S Day; **133** Sousse seen from the Nador tower, AA/S Day; **134tl** Grande Mosquee, Sousse, AA/S Day; **134/135b** Kasbah Sousse Museum, AA/S Day; **135c** Medina, Sousse, AA/S Day; **136** Ribat, Sousse, AA/S Day; **137** Ribat, Sousse, AA/S Day; **138/139** Ribat, Monastir, AA/S Day; **139t** Habib Bourguiba Mausoleum, Monastir, AA; **141** Habib Bourguiba Mausoleum, Monastir, AA/S Day; **142/143t** Ribat, Monastir, AA/S Day; **143b** Ribat, Monastir, AA/S Day; **144** Mosque of Sidi Bou Makhlouf, El Kef, AA/S Day; **144/145** El Kef, AA/S Day; **146l** Grande Mosquee, Mahdia, AA/S Day; **146/147** Borj el Kebir and cemetery, Mahdia, AA/S Day; **148/149** Mahdia, AA/S Day; **149t** Stone carving, Borj el Kebir, Mahdia, AA/S Day; **150/151t** Port El Kantaoui, AA/S Day; **150/151c** Roman ruins, Sbeïtla, AA/S Day; **152/153** Sfax, AA/S Day; **154** Medina, Sfax, G P Bowater/Alamy; **159** Houmt Souq, Isle of Jerba, AA/S Day; **160/161** Sea view, Isle of Jerba, AA/S Day; **162** Potter, Guellala, AA/S Day; **163** Patterned tiles, Guellala, AA/S Day; **164t** Houmt Souq, AA/S Day; **164b** Sailing ship, Houmt Souq, AA/S Day; **165** Souq, Houmt Souq, AA/S Day; **166t** Road near Midoun, AA/S Day; **166/167b** Sidi Mahrez, AA/S Day; **168/169t** Chebika, AA/S Day; **168b** Chott el Jerid, AA/S Day; **169b** Spices, Douz, AA/S Day; **170t** Gabès, AA/S Day; **170bl** Piscines Romaines, Gafsa, AA/S Day; **170/171** Gorges de Selja, AA/S Day; **172tl** Hotel Matmata, AA/S Day; **172/173** Gorge, Midès, AA/S Day; **174** Tamerza, AA/S Day; **175t** Tamerza, AA/S Day; **175c** Tataouine, AA/S Day; **176/177t** Rock faces, Belvedere, Tozeur, Paul Gapper/worldphotos.org/Alamy; **177b** Dar Cheraït Museum, Tozeur, The Tunisian National Tourist Office; **178** Mosquée El Farkous, Tozeur, AA/S Day; **179** Avenue Habib Bourguiba, Tozeur, AA/S Day; **180** Carpet shop, Tozeur, AA/S Day; **181** Palmery, Tozeur, AA/S Day; **182** Camels near Kebili, AA/S Day; **182/183** Chott el Jerid, AA/S Day.

Every effort has been made to trace the copyright holders, and we apologise in advance for any accidental errors. We would be happy to apply the corrections in the following edition of this publication.

Dear Reader

Your comments, opinions and recommendations are very important to us. Please help us to improve our travel guides by taking a few minutes to complete this simple questionnaire.

You do not need a stamp (unless posted outside the UK). If you do not want to cut this page from your guide, then photocopy it or write your answers on a plain sheet of paper.

Send to: **The Editor, AA World Travel Guides,**
FREEPOST SCE 4598, Basingstoke RG21 4GY.

Your recommendations...

We always encourage readers' recommendations for restaurants, nightlife or shopping – if your recommendation is used in the next edition of the guide, we will send you a **FREE AA Guide** of your choice from this series. Please state below the establishment name, location and your reasons for recommending it.

_____

_____

_____

_____

_____

Please send me **AA Guide** _____

About this guide...
Which title did you buy?

AA _____

Where did you buy it?_____

When? m m / y y

Why did you choose this guide? _____

_____

_____

_____

_____

Did this guide meet your expectations?

Exceeded ☐   Met all ☐   Met most ☐   Fell below ☐

Were there any aspects of this guide that you particularly liked? _____

_____

_____

_____

continued on next page...

Is there anything we could have done better? _____
_____
_____
_____

About you...
Name (*Mr/Mrs/Ms*) _____
Address _____
_____
_____ Postcode

Daytime tel nos _____
Email _____

Please only give us your mobile phone number or email if you wish to hear from us about
other products and services from the AA and partners by text or mms, or email.

Which age group are you in?
Under 25 ☐   25–34 ☐   35–44 ☐   45–54 ☐   55–64 ☐   65+ ☐

How many trips do you make a year?
Less than one ☐   One ☐   Two ☐   Three or more ☐

Are you an AA member? Yes ☐   No ☐

About your trip...
When did you book? m m / y y   When did you travel? m m / y y

How long did you stay? _____

Was it for business or leisure? _____

Did you buy any other travel guides for your trip?

If yes, which ones? _____
_____
_____

Thank you for taking the time to complete this questionnaire. Please send it to us as soon as
possible, and remember, you do not need a stamp (*unless posted outside the UK*).

> **AA** Travel Insurance call 0800 072 4168 or visit www.theAA.com